Years of Grace, Life of Mercy

The Story of an Angry Man Who Finds Happiness

Years of Grace, Life of Mercy

The Story of an Angry Man Who Finds Happiness

Larry Caffery

Kravitz & Sons

INNOVATORS IN PUBLISHING, MARKETING AND ADVERTISING

Kravitz and Sons LLC
204 E Arlington Blvd. Suite B
Greenville, NC 27858

Published by Kravitz and Sons LLC.

ISBN: 979-8-89639-733-5 (sc)
ISBN: 979-8-89639-732-8 (e)

Table of Contents

Years of Grace, Life of Mercy

God's GRACE is defined as: Unmerited divine assistance, or unearned and undeserved favor that God shows to humanity through His love and mercy.

God's MERCY is defined as: A compassionate, undeserved kindness that involves withholding punishment and forgiving sin.

Foreword

I sometimes wonder while reading a novel how similar to a particular character the author is and how real to life the character's circumstances are. My sister once had a life-size cardboard cutout of Mickey Spillane posing as his alter ego, Mike Hammer. On the other hand, celebrities are sometimes annoyed by people who mistake them for the fictional character they play. We as readers know to keep the writer and the character distinct in our minds.

The opposite is true, of course, with an autobiography as the two are one and the same. It was a challenge to reconcile the person depicted in the narrative with Larry Caffery, who has been such a caring friend to my husband and me over the years that we have known him and his wife, Glenna. It is as if the Larry he introduced to us no longer exists.

In fact, we are said in Scripture to "put off the old man with his deeds; and put on the new man." Said in another verse to be "after God…created in righteousness and true holiness," this new man is who Larry Caffery is striving to be by the Holy Spirit. So the man described in these pages was, rather than a creation of fiction as it seemed to me, simply the natural man for whom now "old things are passed away, behold all things are become new."

—Katherine Holmes

Introduction

It's 2002, and I'm fifty-two years old. Just last week, I was involved in an incident that I would have reacted differently to just a few years ago. I was driving home from Baltimore, Maryland, on Interstate 70 in my work truck. The person driving in front of me turned onto one of the exit ramps and was completely off the interstate. She decided she had made a wrong turn, and without even looking behind her, she cut across the grass and tried to pull back onto the interstate. My work truck is heavy and doesn't come to a stop quickly. I slammed on my brakes, and my tires were screeching. Everything on my truck seat went flying to the floor. She was now beside me and within inches of my truck.

It was at this time that I was able to look at her and see that she was an elderly lady. As I was trying to stop, she had her gas pedal to the floor. I could tell by the look on her face that she was frightened. She managed to get back onto the interstate in front of me without our vehicles making physical contact.

She still had her gas pedal to the floor and was soon out of my sight. My first impulse was to put my gas pedal to the floor and try to catch up to her. It was only a moment before I realized the absurdity of doing such a thing. I was immediately calm and thought to myself that this was someone's mother and could have just as easily been my mother. She had done something pretty foolish in her driving, but it was an accident, and I was sure her heart was still pounding as a result of what she had done.

I was so preoccupied with what was going on in front of me that I didn't realize the person behind me probably had to slam on his brakes to avoid hitting my truck. However, I was truly amazed at how calm I was. I'm sure I would have responded quite differently just a few years prior. At the very least, I would have attempted to catch up to her and give her some strong words concerning her driving.

I was listening to the Bible on a cassette tape at the time of the incident, and I'm sure that helped me maintain composure. I knew, however, that it was the saving grace of Jesus Christ that had brought about the change in me over the years. Not only was I not angry at the lady, but I prayed for her that she, too, would be calm and that God would protect her in her driving.

My wife of thirteen years and I are active members of Covenant Life Church in Gaithersburg, Maryland. We have two young children, and we take part in the children's ministry program at the church. Most people who know me find it difficult to believe I used to behave in such a different manner. Some might even want to know the formula for change.

There really is no formula, though. It's a matter of daily sanctification (becoming more Christlike). I became a Christian many years ago, but I really had not attained much spiritual growth. At some point, I realized that my life was a mess, and I began to take Christianity more seriously. It was when I began to look to the Bible for answers that my life began to change. I had tried other solutions, but none of them worked. In fact, one of the so-called solutions made my life much worse, even to the point of attempted suicide. This is my story.

*****

This book was written, not as a result of in-depth fact-finding, but rather from mere memory. Therefore, certain dates or sequences of events may be in error. It is the story of my personal life, and no slander or negative remarks are intended against any people mentioned herein.

Book 1

Elementary and Junior High

I believe I am spirit. I am spirit, but for however long God has in mind, I will live in a fleshly body. If we were not spirit, we would not, as told in the Bible, live forever. When I leave this fleshly body, I will continue to exist in yet a new body, I believe, in heaven for all eternity. Some of us will, by our own choosing, spend eternity in hell. So like everyone else on this planet, I was born of a woman.

I came into this world on March 11, 1950. I was the third child and the only son my mother would give birth to. I was named Lawrence after my dad. I was given the middle name Ellis in honor of my mother's brother. I don't know for certain, but I think perhaps my Uncle Ellis was named after Ellis Island when my mother's dad came to America from Canada. My mother's mom died while my mother was still a young child. My mother would give birth to three more daughters.

We lived in Council Bluffs, Iowa. The first house I can remember living in was a small house on Eleventh Street. It was a two-bed-room house with a gas stove that was used for heating the entire house. The foundation of this house was made of small red bricks and was not in great condition. My dad dug a basement under the house. He used a shovel and dug as close to the existing foundation as he thought he safely could. A new foundation was never put in place. We just had a large dirt hole under our house.

I attended kindergarten at Longfellow Public School. I recall that on the first day of kindergarten, I walked three blocks to school by myself. When I arrived at school, I didn't know where to go, so I walked back home. My mother then walked me back to school and got me situated. My kindergarten teacher was Ms. Small. I remember that

Ms.Small was a nice lady, and in spite of her name, she was very large. One day at recess, another boy and I ran into each other head-first. No one at the school noticed. My mother was quite concerned when I arrived home with a large bump on my forehead. For whatever reason, instead of telling my mother what had happened, I told her someone on the playground had thrown a rock and had hit me in the head. I guess even at the tender age of five years, I was too embarrassed to tell my mother what had really happened. The rock story sounded much more heroic. I had probably done so before, but that was the first time I could recall that I had ever lied. My mother telephoned the school and gave them a good scolding, but the school was never able to find the culprit who threw the rock. I have often wondered what story the other youngster had given his parents concerning the bump on his head.

My eldest sister, Linda, was born on May 18, 1947, and was three years older than me. Laura was born on June 24, 1948. On May 1, 1954, Laura died after having suffered several years with polio. I was only four years of age at the time of her death, but I do have some memories of her. I remember that she wore braces on her legs and sat in a wheelchair most of the time. I also remember that she liked to have someone sit on her feet while she was sitting in her wheelchair. She said it made her legs feel better. I recall that I spent some time sitting on Laura's feetv I most likely didn't volunteer to do so.

My family was of the Catholic faith, so when I was ready for the first grade, I attended St. Frances Catholic School. The Catholic school wasn't within walking distance, so my elder sister Linda and I rode the city bus to school. On February 10, 1952, my sister Claudia Jean was born, and on March 21, 1955, my sister Pamela Sue was born. On November 24, 1958, my sister Sharon Lee was born. I was the second eldest of my four surviving sisters, and I didn't take much interest in sports since my dad really had no interest in sports himself.

In 1959, when I was about halfway through the third grade at St. Frances Catholic School, we moved from the east end of town to 3604 Avenue D on the west end of town. I learned that soon after we had moved out of the house at 1812 South Eleventh Street, it was torn down. I didn't recall that the house was in that bad a shape, but apparently, it wasn't worth investing money into the repair of the foundation or worth installing central heating either.

When I was nine, Linda, Claudia, and I started attending Ray F. Meyer Public Elementary School. There were a great number of children living in this new neighborhood, and it proved to be a new experience for me. There must have been close to forty children living in this new neighborhood. I felt as if I was soon put to the test to see what I was made of. I learned that of all these children, I was the quickest on my feet. Phyllis Bly had been the quickest until I came along. I also learned that I was pretty good at wrestling. I liked the new neighborhood, and for a while, I was actually a bit of a bully.

While living in this neighborhood, I had a pet pigeon. When playing down by the Missouri River one day, my friends and I came upon a pigeon that seemed to be tame. I picked it up and carried it home. I found grain along some railroad tracks and had plenty to feed the bird. During the rest of the summer, the pigeon would sit on my handlebars while I rode my bicycle. We had a large maple tree in our yard in which I had a two-story tree house. I made a small cage on the top level and kept the pigeon there.

When winter approached, I put a supply of grain and some water in the cage for the pigeon. One day when I went to check on the bird, it had probably been several weeks, I found that the water was frozen solid, and so was he. I don't suppose it was quite the same as losing a dog or a cat. It's kind of hard to get attached to a pigeon. Anyway, since the bird was dead, I thought it would be nice to have a pigeon skeleton. I put the dead pigeon in an empty lard can and taped another empty lard can to the top. I put the tin can coffin on the basement shelf and waited for several weeks. When I finally opened the cans, I was surprised to see that nothing had happened yet. I decided to speed up the process. I lit my dad's small propane torch and proceeded to burn the feathers and flesh off the bones. It was not long before I heard a yell from my mother, who wanted to know what I was doing to create that horrible smell, which was now throughout the house. The episode was quickly over, and the remains of my pigeon went into the trash.

I finished sixth grade at Ray F. Meyer Elementary School and started what was then called junior high. I rode the bus to Woodrow Wilson Junior High School. Going to a different room for most every class was quite different from grade school, and the days seemed to pass quickly. This was a much larger school, and there was a lot more peer pressure and rivalry.

One day during the first week of school, Jim McTwiggin tried to crowd in front of me while we were in line in physical education class. Jim was bigger than me and probably stronger, but I stood my ground and would not let him in front of me. This was the first but not the last time I had to defend myself from a bully in the years ahead.

I still had little interest or ability in sports, but because I was fast on my feet, I went out for track. By the time I was in the ninth grade, I was doing pretty well at that sport.

I also went out for wrestling and fared okay in that sport as well. In fact, I only lost one wrestling match during the entire season. Yet because I didn't attend the last wrestling match, the coach said I didn't finish the season. So for that reason, even though my picture had been in the local newspaper as an outstanding wrestler, I didn't receive a school letter for that sport. I was really disappointed since I thought it was going to be a sure thing. I had already received a letter sweater from my parents for my birthday, and now I had no school letter to put on it.

At about this same time, my family moved a few blocks to 3234 Avenue C, though I'm not sure why. I think it was probably just to get a lower monthly mortgage payment because it wasn't a move to a better house. There weren't enough bedrooms in the house, so my dad prepared a place for me to sleep in the basement. He put up some paneling for the walls, but the ceiling remained uncovered, so overhead were just rafters and a pull-chain light. I didn't mind, though; at least I had privacy. My mother is still living in that same house some thirty-nine years later.

Back when I was attending Catholic school, I seemed to have some fears. I was never quite sure what I was afraid of, but I would sometimes be on the verge of tears. At some time during my young childhood, my parents had given me a crucifix, probably for my first Communion or confirmation in the Catholic Church. At any rate, the crucifix proved to be a comfort for me as it hung on the wall next to my bed.

For almost as far back as I can remember I wanted to become a Catholic priest. Sometimes when I lay in bed at night and felt fearful, I would put the crucifix under my pillow, but I would also imagine that I was a priest. I imagined myself standing in front of the congregation adorned in my priestly garb. I would imagine that I was saying or performing Mass, and I was comforted. That desire to become a priest stayed with me all the way into high school.

There is at least one fear that is still with me today. I think I know why. Let me tell you some spider stories. Once when I was very young, maybe in kindergarten, I was outside in the garage with my dad. I saw a large spider crawling on the floor and thought it was my duty to step on it. It apparently was carrying an egg sack. At the time, I had no idea what an egg sack was, but all of a sudden, there seemed to me to be hundreds of tiny, little spiders crawling in every direction on the floor. On another occasion, I was standing on the enclosed front porch of our house. It was the Christmas season, and there was a string of lights around the inside doorway to our house. It was dusk, but the lights were on, and there was still enough light so that I could see the spider crawling along the string of lights.

I have to admit that I was curious to see what would happen if the spider crawled into the socket where a bulb was missing. I stood and watched as it did that very thing. All of a sudden, a glowing spider went flying across the front porch; obviously, it had been electro-cuted. It gave me the chills to see such a thing. I was quite thankful that the flying, glowing spider didn't land on me.

On still another occasion when I was several years older, I was delivering newspapers. It was very early on a Sunday morning, and it was still dark. I decided to take a shortcut through a backyard, but not being able to see very well, I walked into a spiderweb. It was the kind of spider that makes a circular web and then sits in the middle of the web, waiting for its prey to get caught. I felt the web on my face and was certain the spider was crawling someplace on my body. I never knew for sure, but I have the chills right now.

One night when I was a seventh grader, about twelve years old, I was lying in bed in the bedroom with the rafters overhead. It was late and dark, but I was still awake. All of a sudden, I felt and heard a plop on my pillow. I flew out of bed like a bolt of lightning and pulled on the chain to the light. There on my pillow sat a large spider, afraid to move. It had apparently been crawling on the rafters over my bed and somehow managed to fall. I was quite chilled, but thankfully, the spider had not landed on my head. And yes, the thought of that gives me chills even now too.

Then another time, when I was much older, at least sixteen years of age, I was sitting behind the wheel in my car with my girlfriend at a drive-in movie. Out of the corner of my left eye, I noticed something. I turned, only to find that one of those large spiders that sits in the middle of its web had made a web in the window opening right next to me. I couldn't imagine how this spider could have spun its web to completion within inches of my head. I was surprised it didn't have its web attached to my head.

Well, I found myself sitting on my girlfriend's lap. I tried to be brave and heroic, but it wasn't easy, as my girlfriend seemed to be unaffected by this spider. I, however, put as much distance between the spider and myself as I could while still remaining in the car. From the passenger seat, where I was now sitting, I picked up a container of popcorn and threw it at the spider. Bull's-eye! Yes! I immediately hopped back over into the driver's seat and rolled up the window. I was thankful my girlfriend was there to comfort me.

I know that many people are fearful of spiders. I'm not sure why; maybe it's because they move so quickly, and they aren't particularly attractive. Anyway, I have to remind myself that everything has a purpose. God created spiders, and He cares about all His creation. I suppose the purpose of spiders is to eat annoying insects like mosquitoes. I'm pretty sure that God didn't create spiders for the purpose of scaring me. I will respect them from a healthy distance.

High School

I did manage to complete the ninth grade at Woodrow Wilson Junior High, and I was now counting down the years—just three more to go. I entered Thomas Jefferson High School for the remainder of my school years. It wasn't easy starting at the bottom again. The seniors liked to tease and bully the sophomores. I didn't go out for track or wrestling in high school, though I did go out for cross-country running when I was in the tenth grade.

As a sophomore, I did quite well. The cross-country team was small, and only five people were allowed to receive a school letter in that sport. All five of these people who received a school letter were seniors, but I as a sophomore, was sixth in line. If I had stayed with it, I am sure I would have done very well in my senior year. I had other interests, though, mainly girls.

When I was in the sixth grade, I was given a hearing test by the school nurse. It was determined that I had a hearing loss in my right ear. My parents took me to an ear, nose, and throat doctor, who decided I needed surgery for an infection of the mastoid bone in my ear. I had the surgery and continued with the hearing loss that never seemed to bother me.

While I was in the tenth grade, my hearing was tested again, and it was suggested that I be seen by a doctor. Once again, my parents took me to the doctor, and the prognosis this time was more serious. The doctor who had performed the surgery on my ear when I was in the sixth grade did not get all the infection cleaned up. Although it never bothered me, and I never had an earache, the infection continued to grow and spread for many years.

The doctor who examined me made arrangements for the second surgery to be done at the University of Iowa Medical Center. A shuttle bus from the hospital came and picked me up at my house and drove me, as well as some other passengers who were picked up along the way, to the hospital in Iowa City, Iowa. I had the surgery, and a couple of days later, the nurse changed my bandage, and I thought I could go home.

I walked down to the train station in town and bought a one-way train ticket to Council Bluffs. By nine that evening, I was back in my house. I had not been home long when the telephone rang. I happened to be the one to answer the phone. After all, I was a teenager and fast on my feet. The call was from the security department at the university hospital. They were quite relieved to learn that I was safe at home. I had apparently been considered a missing patient.

When I was in the tenth grade, it was mandatory that all male students be a part of the ROTC program. I never did know what the letters stood for, but it was military training. One day a week, we were required to wear our military uniform to school and undergo an hour or so of military training. At first, the uniform seemed somewhat of a neat thing, but it grew old quickly. I did not like ROTC! One day at school, I was called out of my class to report to one of the military instructors. He had been going through my school records and learned that I had a hearing loss. He chastised me for not letting him know, and I was dismissed from ROTC permanently. The sergeant told me I would never have to worry about being drafted. Ha! A lot he knew.

Because of my interest in girls and wanting to date, I had to have money, so rather than taking part in sports, I worked after school and on weekends. I obtained a driver's license shortly after my sixteenth birthday. Within a short time, I had my first automobile, a 1957 Chevy purchased at a local car auction for fifty dollars. At that age, I wasn't even close to being mature enough to drive. I drove too fast and gave little consideration to safety.

Driving home one night after dropping off a friend, I had the radio turned up, and I was driving pretty fast. I came to an intersection where the cars from neither direction had a stop sign. While I was in the middle of this intersection, I was hit broadside by someone who had been driving pretty much like me. She was older, though, and should have known better. My car spun around a couple of times, hit a fire hydrant, and knocked it over. Neither of us was given a ticket, and it was never determined who was at fault. Each of us was responsible for our own loss. By the grace of God, I came out of the accident without a scratch and drove more responsibly in the future. I never did well academically. Most of the time, my grades were average or below. I did pretty well during the first semester of my sophomore year, though. Out of five subjects of study, I received four letter grades of A and one B. I could hardly believe it! My parents were really surprised too, but that didn't last long. Between working a part-time job and spending as much time with a girlfriend as I could, there was very little time for doing any studying.

My first real job aside from delivering newspapers was at A&W Root Beer. I flipped a lot of hamburgers and folded a lot of chicken wings. That's right! The chicken wings had to be folded a certain way before they were dipped in batter and deep-fried. Shortly after my sixteenth birthday, I began working at Rog and Scotty's Super Value Store, which was part of a large grocery store chain.

Throughout my years in junior high and my first year in high school, I hadn't had much contact with Jim McTwiggin. Jim McTwiggin, the guy who tried to crowd in front of me in seventh-grade gym class, started working at Super Value shortly after I did. There were no incidents between us.

One day, though, several of us who worked at Super Value, including Jim McTwiggin, were sitting at a counter during our lunch break. Jim was at the opposite end of me. All of a sudden, Jim McTwiggin blurted out, "Caffery, I used to be afraid of you, but I'm not anymore."

That was refreshing news. One of the major concerns in my life for many years had been whether or not Jim McTwiggin was afraid of me. We all ignored Jim, finished our lunch, and went back to work. While I was a senior, a very pretty sophomore girl took a liking to me. Rita Parish was a real knockout, to say the least. What she saw in me, I don't know, but we were soon dating. There was probably not a guy in the entire school who wouldn't have liked to have a date with Rita Parish. Speaking of a knockout, one day, Rita and I were standing in the hall, waiting for our next class to begin, and Rita was pretending to write on my belly with her finger. I was in total la-la land.

Completely without warning, I felt a powerful blow to my mouth. Jim McTwiggin had mustered up enough courage to run up and punch me in the mouth and continue running. A teacher who was standing nearby grabbed me by the arm and tried to hold me, but I easily broke free and went running after Jim. I caught up with him in the boys' room. It had all happened so quickly that I wasn't even sure who had hit me until I was standing face-to-face with Jim. He was standing there with his hands up, ready to defend himself. I couldn't help but think how pitiful he looked and said, "Jim, you're not worth the trouble," then I walked away.

That evening, Jim telephoned me at home to apologize. He told me that he was jealous because I was dating Rita, and he thought that I was more of a man than he would ever be. I thought it was pretty manly of him to call and tell me that, but I didn't tell him. That was my last episode with Jim McTwiggin.

During my high school years, I decided I wanted to become a Catholic priest. I somehow became connected with a Catholic seminary on the other side of the state, and a priest there invited me to come out and spend a weekend so they could evaluate me as a possible student, and I could check out the seminary as well. So with my parents' permission, one early morning, I boarded a Greyhound bus and began the long trip across the state of Iowa, to the town of Epworth, to the Divine Word Seminary. One of the priests met me at the bus station and drove me to the seminary.

During my interview, a concern about my low grades in school was brought up. The fact that I had received a few letter grades of A was appealing to them, though. They decided that if my desire was strong and I applied myself and worked very hard, I would be able to make it through seminary.

However, by the end of my two-day visit, my desire to be a priest was gone. In that short time, I realized that the priesthood was not for me. I was a rather shy, quiet person, and I guess I thought anyone wanting to become a priest would be a lot like me. Not so. Most of the students there were active in sports and were outgoing. They didn't appear to take their relationships with God as seriously as I took mine. I just didn't seem to fit in. Although I did have a heart for the Lord at a young age, I think my desire to become a priest was based more on the prestige of the position and perhaps the idea of wearing colorful clothing. I also realized that to become a priest, I would have had to give up dating. I continued in the Catholic Church but never again gave any thought to becoming a priest.

Because I did have a heart for the Lord, high school was sometimes difficult for me. I pretty much hung out with the same friends I had in junior high all the way through high school. I never kept it a secret that I wanted to become a priest, but I think my friends never took me seriously. I'm sure the fact that I liked to date didn't help. Although I was not sexually active during most of my high school years, some of my friends thought it funny that I wanted to become a priest. Sometimes when they were going to go out on a Friday evening, they would exclude me because they thought I would not take part in their misbehavior and would spoil their fun.

On an occasion or two, I did go out with them and got drunk. After I returned from my visit to the seminary and told of my experience there, that saga was over, although they still sometimes excluded me from their gatherings. Peer pressure made life difficult for me, and I was glad when high school was completed.

After graduating from high school, I started attending a business college to learn how to become a computer programmer. It took only four weeks for me to decide that computers were not for me. I dropped out of the business college and applied for a job at Precision Optics Inc. in Omaha, Nebraska. I was nervous about the interview and did not expect to be hired. Mr. Woodford, the owner of Precision Optics Inc., was concerned that if he hired me, I would soon be drafted into the military, and the time and money he spent training me would be a loss. I explained to him that I was discharged from ROTC in high school because of loss of hearing in my right ear and would not have to serve in the military. Mr. Woodford suggested to me that I volunteer for the draft. He suggested that I go to the marines because their physical exam is tougher than the army's, and I would be more likely to fail the exam.

I followed his advice and went to the US Marines' recruiting office, where I failed the physical exam due to my hearing loss. Mr. Woodford then hired me under the assumption that I would never be drafted. I would now be learning how to manufacture contact lenses, and I was sure I would never be serving any time in the military.

One Friday evening when I was out with one of my friends from high school, I met a girl named Candy Smith at one of the local teen hangouts. She was three years younger than me and had just finished junior high. That didn't matter to me, though. I thought she was gorgeous! She gave me her telephone number, and I telephoned her the very next day. We began to date each other and were becoming very close.

The starting pay at Precision Optics Inc. was not great, but I was happy about getting the job. I was required to wear a dress shirt and necktie to work. I also wore a white lab coat. I had to learn to use the metric system, which proved to be easier than I had anticipated. I just took it a day at a time, thinking that each day I went to work would be my last. I never got fired, though. I made it through the probationary period and was doing pretty well.

I had been working for Precision Optics Inc. for about six months when I received a letter from the local draft board. The letter said,

> Greetings, your friends and neighbors have
> selected you to serve in the U.S. Army.

I thought it had to be a joke, and I wanted to find my friends and neighbors who were responsible.

I soon found out that it was no joke! The US Marines did not want me, but the US Army did. The Vietnam War was still going strong in 1969, and the army apparently had lowered its standard. I had only a couple more weeks before I was inducted into the US Army. Then on June 6, 1969, I said goodbye to Candy and family, and I was on my way.

Military Life

I flew to Fort Leonard Wood in Missouri for my basic training. To say I hated the military would be an understatement! Upon our arrival at the induction station, we had our first experience with being shouted at. While standing in line, a drill sergeant approached me. With his nose next to mine, he shouted, "Where are you from, trooper?"

I shouted back, "Sergeant, I'm from Council Bluffs, Iowa, Sergeant!"

Another drill sergeant stepped up and yelled, "Council Bluffs? Isn't that where the marines ship all their dead pissants?"

Making fun of my hometown really didn't bother me, though. I was bothered when they said there was a church on base if any of us sissies thought we wanted to go on Sunday morning. What really made me angry was the fact that no one had warned me what to expect.

The only person who had said anything to me was Mr. Woodford. He told me that the main thing was to just do what I was told.My dad had been in the army for five years, so I couldn't understand why he hadn't tried to prepare me for what to expect. The idea of the military training was to put everyone on the same level and treat everyone the same no matter what walk of life he came from. We were all treated the same all right! We were all treated like dirt, at least while in basic training.

I missed Candy more than I ever thought possible, and I was just plain miserable. I thought I was in pretty good physical condition when I got out of high school, but the physical training offered by the army really put me to the test, although it did get easier as the days went by. I never liked it. I think was just learning to live with it. I considered myself to be a pacifist at that time, and I had no desire to learn how to shoot an M14 rifle. One day when we were at the rifle range, I had an exchange with the drill sergeant⊠ There was a row of foxholes at the rifle range. Each of us trainees was down in a foxhole, and we were supposed to shoot at the target that represented Vietnamese soldiers. The army was trying to make a killer out of me, and I did not appreciate it! I simply fired my weapon without aiming at the target. The drill sergeant came up behind me and kicked me in the shoulder. He shouted something to me about shooting at the target. I was angry, and my first thought was to turn my weapon on him. If he wanted me to be a killer, he could be my first victim, but by the grace of God, I didn't do what I felt like doing.

I somehow managed to bluff my way through. When my eight weeks of training were complete, I almost dreaded going home. It was tough leaving home for the first time to enter the military when I didn't really know what to expect, but now I did! I knew it would be very difficult to go home to freedom and friends and then have to leave again in two weeks. I knew it would be especially difficult to leave Candy. In some ways, I would have preferred to have just stayed there and not go back home until my two years in the army were completed. We were told by one drill sergeant, however, that the army would be a lot different once we were out of basic training. At some time during my eight weeks of basic training, I took a battery of tests to determine what I was most skilled to do. On one of the many forms I filled out, I was asked what I would like to do or what my interests were. I didn't think it would make any difference, but I checked off electronics, although I didn't have computers in mind. Just before I left Fort Leonard Wood in Missouri, I received my new orders. In two weeks, I was supposed to report to Redstone Arsenal in Huntsville, Alabama, for my next course of training. I was going to be trained as a computer repairman for the Pershing Missile System.

My two weeks of freedom passed more quickly than I could have imagined. Saying goodbye to Candy was extremely difficult. I don't know exactly when it happened, but Candy and I decided to get married. Because I was a devout Catholic, I would not have married Candy unless she became a Catholic, so while I was in Alabama, Candy took the Catholic convert class and became a member of the Catholic denomination.

When I arrived at Redstone Arsenal, I was surprised at how different I was treated in comparison to my arrival at basic training. I was actually welcomed and treated as a human being. I was not a happy camper, though. After all, I had dropped out of computer school due to a lack of interest and understanding. I considered myself to be a pacifist, and now I was going to be taught how to use computers in conjunction with ballistic missiles.

I didn't do well in school. It's a little different in the army than in a civilian school though. If you're not making the grade, you don't flunk the class. Instead, the army just puts you back at the beginning with a new class that's starting. They call it being recycled.

The computer class I was assigned to was supposed to last six and a half months. I was recycled twice before I finally made it through. Part of my problem was that I really didn't understand a lot of what was being taught, and another part of my problem was my attitude. I really didn't want to be there, and I didn't really care about the school. Anyway, because I was recycled twice in what was supposed to be a six-and-a-half-month program, I was there for at least nine months. My two years of military obligation was slowly dwindling down.

I remained strong in my faith while in Alabama, and I attended the Catholic Church service every Sunday. Candy and I wrote and talked to each other as often as we could. She was busy taking the Catholic convert classes and making arrangements for our wedding.I was released from my obligations at Redstone Arsenal in Huntsville, Alabama, and had two weeks of leave before I was to report for duty in Germany. Although I had been drafted and was serving in the military, I was not of legal age to get married and needed permission from my parents. Candy needed permission also, but our parents had no problem with us getting married, so we took our permission notes from our mommas and daddies and obtained our marriage license. No one could have told me then, but I can say it now. If you need permission from your mommy and daddy to get married, you have no business getting married. Candy was only seventeen, and I had just turned twenty.

On May 9, 1970, Candace Charlene Smith and I became husband and wife. Our honeymoon was short, and I was soon boarding a plane for Germany. I had promised Candy that I would make arrangements for her to come and live with me in Germany as soon as I could.

When I arrived in Germany, I was placed in the unit with the guys I had originally started with in computer school. They had already been there for three months, and it was reassuring to be with some people I already knew. Ray Bogus and I had become pretty good friends when we were in Alabama. I ended up bunking in a room with Ray and two other guys I did not yet know. It was mandatory for all new arrivals in Germany to stay on base until completing an orientation class on German culture. It was my first night there, but Ray and I had no intention of staying on base. We went to the back of the base, away from the main gate, where we waited for the security guard to go past. Then we hightailed it over the fence, barbed wire and all.

Walking through the streets of Germany for the first time was pretty exciting. I didn't know a word of German, of course, but because of the military base, there were a lot of Americans around. Many of the German people were able to speak some English. Anyway, Ray and I took a walking tour of the town of Neckarsulm and returned to base through the front gate.

For whatever reason, the military used different personal service identification numbers to distinguish between those who enlisted and those who were drafted. For those who were drafted, the numbers were preceded by *US*. My number, for example, was US 56548526. If you enlisted, your number was preceded by the letters *RA*.

Everyone's name and identification number were printed in bold black lettering on his duffel bag. When I arrived at the military base in Neckarsulm, Germany, my duffel bag was taken off the bus and placed in the hall of the barracks I would be staying in. Most everyone in the barracks was curious to see who the new arrival was, so they checked out the number on my duffel bag. That's how Ray Bogus discovered I was there and tracked me down in the office where I was waiting for a room assignment.

One of the first things the guys noticed was my US identification number. They all knew I had been drafted. Most of the guys had already been on that base for a year or more, and I would be leaving before they did. Some of them were downright angry about that. Apparently, the computer school I had attended (and didn't care anything about) was a prestigious school, and there was a waiting list to get into it. No one there particularly liked the army, and they were all eager to get out! Most of them were angry because they had to enlist for three years to get into this school, and I was drafted for only two years of service. It wasn't my fault, I certainly didn't tell any of them to enlist, but some of them took their anger out on me. Some of them snubbed me for a long time.

I don't recall how long I had to live in the barracks until I was able to get a place off base and send for Candy. It seemed like a very long time. It was difficult because most everyone on the base used drugs. The nickname for the popular drug was hash. I never did know for sure what it was, although I remember that it was a brown powder. I think it was supposed to be smoked, but Ray Bogus would sometimes pour some into the soda he was drinking. It may be difficult to believe, but I knew of only four people in the entire barracks, including myself, who were not doing drugs.

Because I didn't do drugs and because I had been recycled in school twice and arrived three months behind the rest of my class, some of the guys believed I was a narc and avoided me like the plague. A narc was someone who had been trained to detect drug use and was basically a stool pigeon or a squealer. I, of course, was not a narc. I can't tell you how many lives I've seen ruined because of drug use, including the life of my friend. We were paid once a month, and Ray, as well as many others, would spend their entire paycheck on drugs. Most of the time, I was left alone in the barracks.

On one occasion, I felt I could not take it anymore, and I went out with Ray Bogus and some others. We all bought a soda, and I let Ray pour some hash into mine. Everyone was waiting to see what effect it would have on me. They were all equally amazed when they saw no change in my behavior. Ray was in total disbelief. He said, "I gave you enough hash to stone a cow!"

Most of them thought I was really weird.

On yet another occasion when I was feeling very lonely, I accepted an invitation. Some guys were going somewhere to smoke pot in their car. I went along and took part. I don't recall if I was affected by whatever it was. As it turned out, the idea of inviting me was just a test so they could determine whether or not I was a narc. Because I went along and took part, they decided that I wasn't, but I still didn't fit in.

There was a Catholic Church on the base where I attended Mass every Sunday morning. The crowd was always very small, and I was the only one from my entire unit to attend. I really missed Candy, and I was still eager for her to come to Germany. I didn't have enough rank to qualify for a house off base. Candy and I would have to live on the German economy. I did finally get money saved for Candy's airfare and was able to find us a small apartment just two blocks from the base. There was no way we would be able to afford a car and pay rent too, so it was a real blessing living so close to the base.

Another married guy in my unit started to befriend me because his wife was already with him, and he was looking for a companion for her. The big day finally arrived and Jerry Kemple and his wife, Gloria, took me to the airport in Frankfurt to pick up Candy. I was glad, too, that Candy was able to meet Gloria. It's not easy living on the German economy when you can't speak any German. Our landlord and his wife were very nice, but communication with them was next to impossible. We knew how much our rent was and when it was due. That's all that was necessary.

Candy and I hadn't lived together as husband and wife until now. Fortunately, there was no help or interference from other family members, and we were on our own. Unfortunately, neither Candy nor I had had good role models as we were growing up. We hadn't received any premarital counseling, and we really didn't know how a married couple should treat each other. Candy and I disagreed and argued with each other a lot even when we were dating. I guess we just thought it was normal behavior. We continued to do so while living in Germany. I was very critical of her. She was very pretty, intelligent, and well-mannered. She took good care of herself and always looked nice, but I could always find some fault to complain about. Candy was probably unhappy with the situation, but I don't recall that she ever said so.

While I was serving in Germany, I still considered myself to be a pacifist. I really hated being there, and I did not cooperate. On one occasion, we were supposed to go to the rifle range to requalify with the M14 rifle. I went to the commanding officer, Major Nelson, and told him I was not going to go. I didn't really tell him what my feelings or beliefs were. I was very bold, though, and I told him I was already deaf in one ear, and I was not going to risk damaging the hearing in my other ear. He told me I would have to go. He got out his personal earplugs in their little container and handed them to me. I did go to the rifle range, but when everyone else got out of the truck, I stayed behind. No one missed me, and whoever was responsible for checking the target I had supposedly shot at marked me down as having done well.

I was awarded a Sharp Shooter Medal with the M14 rifle. It's rather funny, I think. According to my military records, I was also awarded a Good Conduct Medal and a National Defense Service Medal. I did receive the medals, but it was all bogus. A few days after returning from the rifle range, I was walking around the base with a couple of other guys. We happened to come upon Major Nelson, who was standing and visiting with another officer. I threw the container of earplugs at him, which landed at his feet. I shouted, "Your earplugs, sir!" then turned and walked away. He said nothing to me. The time passed slowly, but I was now down to only three more months. When a person was down to only three months, it was the practice to take his green fatigue hat, set it on top of his boots, and take a photograph. I did so. I was now officially short!

One day, we were greeted at our morning formation by a new first sergeant. He referred to us as *peons*. I didn't know what that meant, but it didn't sound good to me. It sounded degrading! Apparently, some of the guys complained to the company commander. A few days later, the first sergeant apologized to us. He said *peon* was common lingo in his former company, and no one seemed to mind.

Major Nelson wanted to see me in his office. I reported immediately. He told me I was being transferred to Headquarters Company, where I was going to become a part of the unit police and be a gate guard. I was just counting down my time, so it didn't make any difference to me. It did, however, turn out to be a good duty, and many in my old unit were envious of me. They had to go past me every day that I was on duty at the main gate to the base. I worked eight-hour shifts. I had two days of A shift, two days of B shift, one night of C shift, and had the next full week off. It was easy but boring.

Candy and I never did get a car, so we couldn't travel, but we had seen everything within walking distance many times. One day, as I reported for my shift, a military vehicle was going out the gate just as I was stepping into the guardhouse. It was exactly 5:00 p.m. The driver of this vehicle did not have proper clearance to leave the base. He went out and got drunk and wrecked the vehicle. The guard commander tried to make me responsible for letting the driver out of the gate. I had not yet begun my shift, and I refused to accept responsibility.

I was presented with an Article 15. An Article 15 is a type of military punishment in which the guilty party is fined, and the money is taken out of his paycheck. There was a catch, though. The punishment cannot be administered unless the soldier signed the Article 15, which is an admission of guilt. I, of course, refused to sign anything. The commander of the guard advised me that if I didn't sign the Article 15, the only alternative was a court-martial, which is a military trial. He reminded me that I had only two months remaining and told me that if I was court-martialed, my stay would be increased. I still refused to sign.

The matter was apparently dropped, and I received orders giving me a one-month early discharge. We made arrangements, and Candy flew back to the United States. I spent my very boring last month in Germany by myself. The two weeks I had off were almost unbearable. I didn't like to read, and there was no television. I wondered how Candy had spent so much time alone in that little apartment.

My day finally arrived. I had to report to my former company commander, Major Nelson, who had to sign my separation papers.

He did so without a problem, smiled, and said, "I knew you'd do a good job as a gate guard."

I was flown back to Fort Dix, New Jersey, on May 27, 1971, and I was given an honorable discharge from the US Army.

Back in the USA

Candy and I were now living in an apartment owned by and upstairs from her grandparents. The apartment was not much larger than the one we had in Germany, but it was so good to be back with Candy and back in the United States that it didn't matter. We had only been back in the States for about a month when we learned that Candy was pregnant, so I went back to work for the optical company, Precision Optics Inc. I had new responsibilities now and knew I had to work hard and save money.

I was doing well at work, and Candy and I were able to move into a larger apartment before our child was born. It was a pretty new apartment complex called Place 35. It just so happened that the husband of the lady responsible for renting out the units was in the military at that time. There was a waiting list to get in, but because I had been in the military, we were given priority. On January 9, 1972, Michael Scott was born. I was thrilled to have a son, but it seemed unbelievable to me that I could be a parent. Candy had been working before Mike was born and continued to do so afterwards for about a year. One of Candy's grandmothers was taking good care of Mike, but I decided that it was my responsibility to be the breadwinner, and I wanted Candy to stay home and take care of him. Even with Candy not working outside our home, we were able to save enough money to make a down payment on a house. We bought a single-family house for $12,500. It was a small two-bedroom house, but it was large enough for us at that time.

Mr. Woodford, at Precision Optics Inc., was a hard man to work for. I always knew where I stood with him, and I liked that. It was my opinion, however, that he did not treat people well. Most of the employees were female, and Mr. Woodford frequently had one or the other of them in tears. He shouted at people and often put people down, sometimes calling someone stupid or lazy. At this time, I had been working for Mr. Woodford for several years and had seen a lot of people come and go.

One day, he really ticked me off. I didn't say anything to him, but I displayed a very defiant attitude. For the most part, I was ignoring him, even when he spoke to me. After several days of this, he had lost patience with me. He told me very firmly to follow him to his office. I could tell by the expression on most everyone's face that they thought I was going to be fired. I did too! At this point, though I was still so angry with him, I did not really care. He was on one side of his big mahogany desk, and I sat across from him on the other side. As I recall, I was actually fired, but before I left his office, I was rehired. At some point, he made a comment about people not wanting to work. He said, "What's wrong with people?"

I very firmly replied, "Don, it's not them. It's you! You don't know how to treat people!"

That type of behavior was completely out of character for me. No one ever talked back to Don Woodford, and hearing it from me really caught him off guard. For a moment, he just sat there with his mouth open, as if in shock. I was rather surprised at myself. I would never have spoken to him in such a manner if I had not been very angry.

After that, the tone in the room changed. He actually apologized and told me he would try to be a better boss. I think he forgot that he had fired me, and before I left his office, I was not only still employed but had been offered any position in the contact lens lab that I wanted. We agreed that in the future, I would do only specialty work. And just for the record, from that day on, he was a better boss. Although I didn't particularly like school and didn't do very well, I decided I wanted to take advantage of my military benefits and go to college. I talked with one of the counselors at Metropolitan Technical Community College in Omaha. The college offered a two-year associate degree program in ophthalmic technology. The ophthalmic program was supposedly one of the more difficult programs the college offered. Based on my high school grades, the counselor suggested the course might be too difficult for me. I assured him I was enthusiastic and would be able to do the work. He reluctantly let me enroll in the program. I applied for my military benefit to go to college and was given approval. I never thought I'd be excited about going to school, but I was. I was going to go to college, and the government was going to pay all my expenses! I was going to work my full-time job during the day and attend college part-time in the evenings.

On the first night of class, there were forty-one students in the classroom. The ophthalmic professor, Mr. Pleasant Lewallen, informed us that the class was too large. He said he preferred to have a class of about fifteen students. He then told us that by the end of the first week, at least half of us would be gone. He certainly put a fear in me. I guess he was trying to find out who was really serious about the program and to weed everyone who wasn't. I was beginning to have doubts that I would survive, but I was determined to make it all the way through. Mr. Lewallen did know what he was talking about. At the beginning of the second week, the class was only about one-half the size it started out, but I was still there. I had survived the first week!

During this time period, Candy again became pregnant, and on March 31, 1974, she gave birth to our second son. We named him Steven David. Once again, I was thrilled with having a son. We now had two sons. Life was good. Candy and I still argued quite a lot, but our problems did not seem to be serious, and I thought our marriage was as good as most.

The house we were living in stood on a four-foot foundation. It had what was called a four-foot crawl space. I decided I would dig down another five feet, and we would then have a full basement or what would be called a shelf basement. So while I was still working full-time and going to school three evenings a week, I also began digging a basement with the shovelful! I worked hard in college and did very well. Having an interest in what I was studying seemed to really make a difference.

We were doing pretty well financially because in addition to my paycheck, we were receiving several hundred dollars a month from the federal government. This money was above and beyond all my college expenses, so we were able to save some money.

On the evenings I didn't have school, I would come home from work, eat dinner, and immediately begin working at digging out my basement. I was always busy and felt I was accomplishing a lot. What

I failed to realize was that I was neglecting my family. Unfortunately, it would be several years before I would make that realization.

At the end of the fourth quarter of college I had a 4.0 grade average. Not only was I still in the program, but I was doing better than anyone else in the class. During the last quarter of college, it was required of each of us that we work a part-time job for an optical company manufacturing spectacles.

This posed a real problem for me. I had a very nice, well-paying job manufacturing contact lenses, yet Mr. Lewallen insisted that I would not receive my college degree unless I did as he required.I knew he was wrong, and I was very angry. Ophthalmic was ophthalmic; it didn't make any difference what type of lenses were being manufactured, studied, etc.

I talked with a school counselor, who agreed with me that the entire ophthalmic program at the college could just have easily been taught using contact lenses as spectacle lenses, yet he also said Mr. Lewallen's decision would stand. Now I was really angry. I was not about to be denied the associate degree I had worked so hard for because of some silly idea.

One evening, I went to the school early and met Mr. Lewallen in his office. Anger was controlling me. Within seconds, we were shouting at each other. I went over and shut his door so no one could hear us. He could see how angry I was, and he appeared to be very nervous. I stood firm and insisted that I would not let him ruin my work career. He finally consented to let me use my current ophthalmic job to fulfill my obligation.

One day while I was working, I looked up and saw Mr. Lewallen walking and talking with my employer. He had come to do my work experience evaluation. The next evening in class, he asked me if I had seen him there. I told him I had. He then said, "Boy, they sure like you!" He gave me an A for my work experience obligation.

Because I was going to college part-time, it took me three years to complete the program. By the end of the third year, there were only five of us remaining in the class. I not only finished the program and earned my associate degree, but I was the valedictorian of that particular ophthalmic class.

I continued to use most of my spare time digging my basement. It was almost equivalent to digging several basements. I had to move all the dirt several times. I would throw dirt out of an opening I had made in the foundation and make a large pile in the backyard. I would then shovel the dirt in my pickup truck and haul it off. I had no problem finding places to put the dirt. There was always someone wanting free dirt. It took me at least three years to complete the project. When I was finished digging, I hired someone to come and put up concrete blocks and pour a concrete floor. The house remained on its original foundation. I had a three-foot-wide concrete shelf at the bottom of the original foundation and then a new wall at the edge of the shelf.

Some of my friends and neighbors thought I had gone off the deep end, having undertaken such a project. It didn't stop me, though. I probably never felt better than I did while on a regular routine of digging. After all, I was certainly getting a lot of exercise while I was digging. The entire project only cost me several thousand dollars and proved to pay a nice dividend.

One day when I arrived home from work, my two-year-old son, Mike, met me at the front door. He was very excited. He said he had seen Jesus, and Jesus had said, "Die, die, die."

Once I got into the house, Candy explained what had happened. Candy told me that Mike claimed to have seen Jesus standing by a particular chair in our living room. Jesus had said to him, "Die, die, die." This event had happened early in the day, and Candy said Mike had been excited and kept telling of the experience all day long. Candy was concerned, and I was too. As Catholics, we went to church on a regular basis, and when we prayed, it was just a form of prayer that we had memorized. The name of Jesus was seldom, if ever, used. We had no idea what to make of the situation.

Several months later, I received a phone call at work. I was told that it was my wife and that she sounded very upset. Mike was going to go into the hospital to have some dental work done. Candy had taken him to the University of Nebraska Hospital for a pre-entrance exam. The doctor who examined Mike told Candy in a very cold, harsh manner that Mike had a tumor on one of his kidneys and was probably going to die. That is what Candy had called to tell me.

I left work immediately and went home. We took Mike to the University of Nebraska Hospital and had him admitted for testing. Mike was soon diagnosed with a Wilms' tumor, which is a fast-growing cancerous tumor of the kidney. Mike remained hospitalized and underwent surgery for complete removal of his right kidney. As I recall, the doctors believed the tumor had not yet metastasized (spread), but they wanted Mike to undergo chemotherapy as a precaution.

Candy and I were told that Mike would do fine with one kidney. His remaining kidney would become enlarged to compensate for the lost kidney. We were told also that they were not sure what caused the Wilms' tumor. They said they thought it was either inherited from the mother's side of the family, or perhaps it was caused by a blow to the kidney.

When I heard that news, I nearly collapsed. I was sure that I was the cause of Mike's illness. I immediately recalled a time when I was spanking Mike in anger. I was sure that I had hit him too hard, and although I was aiming for his little bare bottom, my aim was high. I hadn't given it much thought at the time, but after hearing what the doctor mentioned as a possible cause, I was sure I had hit Mike in the kidney. I lived with that guilt for many year.

Mike was just three years of age when his kidney was removed, and chemotherapy was started right away. The chemotherapy caused Mike to lose his hair. At the age of three, that was not a significant factor, and his hair soon grew back. Over the next six years, Mike would be in and out of the hospital with continued chemotherapy and blood transfusions. The doctors continued to check Mike for any signs of new cancer. He seemed to remain in remission, but because he was a growing boy, it was believed that it was best to keep him on a regular regimen of chemotherapy until he was through his teen years. I believe Mike received chemotherapy every six months or so. Now that he was older and in school, it was more difficult to deal with his hair loss. Candy and I purchased a hairpiece for him to wear, but he preferred not to. One day shortly after school was out, Mike's younger brother, Steve, came running into the house, nearly out of breath. He told us that some kids were teasing Mike, calling him baldy. I wanted to run and rescue Mike, but I knew I couldn't. I felt like hurting the kids who were teasing Mike, but I could not do that either. All we could do was endure the best we could.

Candy once again became pregnant, and on April 15, 1979, Timothy Sean was born. Candy and I now had three wonderful sons. Still, I would have been happy to have been blessed with a daughter. Candy and I had to be separated from our two youngest sons periodically. While Mike was in the hospital for chemotherapy, Steve and Tim would stay in Thurman, Iowa, with Candy's parents. It was very stressful for Candy and me. I was concerned about neglecting Steve and Tim, so Candy and I seldom went out together.

Our relationship was not great, and we decided to get some counseling for ourselves. The counseling we received was at the veterans' hospital in Omaha. It was another benefit of my having served in the military. I did have a problem dealing with anger, and that was one of the things we were working on. The counseling seemed to be of little help. One day, our counselor telephoned us at home. He told us one of his sons had been in a serious accident and may die. He was distraught and said he understood now that the bulk of the problems Candy and I were having was due to the illness of our son. It was indeed very stressful.

I was still dealing with anger very poorly, and I'm sure there were many occasions when I frightened Candy. I recall one occasion that I really made a fool of myself. Council Bluffs, Iowa, was a railroad town, so it was frequent to have to wait for a train to pass while driving. At this time, Candy was pregnant with Mike. She and I were in our car together, approaching a large section of railroad tracks. The road was still open, but I saw a train coming. I decided that I would make the train stop and wait for me for a change, so I pulled onto the train tracks and stopped the car. I was pretending that the car had stalled. I was certain the train engineer could see my car on the track, but he was making no effort to stop the train. The train was moving slowly, but it was obvious that he planned on hitting us. I got the car started and out of the way just in time. Now I was really angry!

I jumped out of the car, ran to catch up with the engine, and when I did, I saw three men on board. I didn't care, though. I was prepared to take all three of them on! I took hold of the stair railings and proceeded to pull myself up. I had only made it up two of the four steps, when I caught an engineer boot in my chest. The kick had knocked me off the train and left me with a fractured rib. I then looked back and saw that

I had about a half mile to walk back to my car. Candy was speechless and, I'm sure, quite terrified!

There was yet another occasion at the same intersection. This time, the train already had the intersection blocked, and it was at a complete stop. Candy and I were the first ones in the line of cars. I had waited long enough. I could see the train engine, so I jumped out of my car and ran toward it.

When I got there, I saw two men on the engine and a third very young man standing at a switching lever about twenty feet in front of the train. The two men on board were leisurely visiting while the third man seemed to be at a complete loss as to what he was supposed to do.I began screaming at the men on the train and shouted to them, "My wife is pregnant, and I need to get her to the hospital, and you'd better get this son-of-a-bitch train moving, and I mean now!"

They began shouting orders at the younger man, about my age, who was still trying to figure out what he needed to do. I turned and headed back to my car. By the time I got back, the train was already moving at a pretty good clip.

On another occasion—no trains involved—I made a fool of myself once again. Candy and I had hired a company to put new custom-made storm windows on our house. After all, we were living in Iowa, where winters are very cold! They had completed the job, with the exception of two windows. Several weeks had passed, and they still had not returned to finish the job. Cold weather was fast approaching, and I decided to give them one more week. They didn't show.

One Friday evening after work, I drove to their manufacturing plant in Omaha, walked into the business office, sat down like I owned the place, and began to demand to know when they were going to finish the job on my house. When the telephone rang, I answered it and said, "I'm sorry but we're closed now."

They then threatened to call the police. I told them to go ahead and do so, that they could probably use the publicity. They finally told me they would finish my two windows and install them the next day. I was satisfied and left. It's really amazing to me what a quiet, shy person like me will do when he is motivated by anger. Just for the record, I did finally get it under control but not as of yet.

On the brighter side, let me tell you a hog story. I was a city boy to be sure. One day, Candy and I were visiting her parents on their small farm in Thurman, Iowa. It had been raining, and the entire place was a mire of mud. When the rain stopped, my father-in-law told me to come with him to help feed the hogs. I waded through the mud with him to the pigsty. There must have been at least ten hogs romping around in the mud. My father-in-law pointed to the pigsty and said, "Hop in there and turn that one over while I go get a sack of feed."

I tried to keep my eye on the hog I thought he had pointed to, but I couldn't imagine why he wanted me to hop into that mud hole and try to wrestle a pig and turn it over. I thought he had lost it! I wondered if he planned on force-feeding this hog or what! Anyway, I decided that I wasn't about to wrestle a hog in the mud, and I wouldn't have hopped over that fence even if it had been dry.

By now my father-in-law was on his way back, carrying a sack of feed that was slung over his shoulder. He shouted to me, "Did you get that one turned over?"

"No," I replied. "I don't know which one it is."

He came up to me and looked at me like he thought I was crazy. He said, "Why, it's that one right there!"

I then looked down and saw the corner of a feed trough, which was just barely sticking out of the mud. He hopped over the fence, turned over the trough, and filled it with feed. I never did tell him how close I came to hopping over that fence to wrestle one of his hogs to the ground. If I had, he would surely have thought I was crazy and most likely would have been correct in his assessment. I can see it now. I'd have probably been shouting, "Hurry, I can't hold him much longer!"

He may have been shouting, "Hey, what are you trying to do to my hog?"

While Candy was still pregnant with our third child, we decided we would need a larger house. We put our house on the market, the one we bought for $12,500. It didn't take long to sell, and it sold for a little over $27,000. The time I had spent digging the basement paid off even better than I had expected. We now had enough money to have a new three-bedroom house built and enough left to buy a second house to use as a rental property. It took about three months to get the new house built, and about three weeks after Tim was born, we moved to 3508 Katie Drive.

We met our next-door neighbors on Katie Drive. They were about the same age as Candy and me. Their names were Sharon and Harry Elliott. Sharon was attractive but not more so than Candy. Candy and I were still struggling in our marriage, though, and when Sharon began to show interest in me, it was difficult for me to resist her. Candy was working for Federal Express, and on one particular evening, she was attending a company dinner. Spouses were invited, but Candy didn't want me to go because she thought I might get angry and make a scene.

I was feeling pretty depressed. Candy's mother was visiting us at the time, so she was there to watch our children. I received a phone call from Henry Elliott. He and his wife wanted me to come over and drink a few beers with them. Being lonely and depressed, I decided I would.

Sharon and Harry continued to insist that I drink more. As it turned out, they had a plan. Harry had agreed to let Sharon and me have sex together. He had reasoned in his own mind that I would then owe him, and he would be able to have sex with my wife. In my drunken stupor, I ended up in bed with Sharon. I had committed adultery!

The next day, when I recalled what had happened, I could hardly live with myself. Late that afternoon, when Candy and our sons left in the car, Sharon telephoned me. She must have been watching for the car to leave. She wanted to know if I wanted to come over and do it again. The Holy Spirit had strongly convicted me of my sin, and my answer to Sharon was no. I told her I felt terrible about what had happened. She said she was afraid of that. I vowed to never get drunk or commit adultery again. I have not. As it turned out, Harry Elliott and Candy were both working for Federal Express. When Harry finally realized Candy had no interest in him and that he was not going to be able to be with her, he began to harass her at work. I didn't appreciate him messing with my wife. One day when I saw him pull into his driveway, I ran out to meet him. I'm not really sure what my intention was, but I got physical with him. When he saw me coming, he decided to stay in his car. I opened the door and tried to pull him out. He turned and lay on his back and was kicking at me with his feet and screaming for his wife to call the police. I thought it best that I go back into my house. It wasn't long before the police were knocking on my door.

I told the police officer what had happened. He just shrugged his shoulders and left. I don't even know if he bothered to write a report. A few days later, the local sheriff showed up at my door to present me with a court summons. Harry had filed assault and battery charges against me. The sheriff told me it was a serious offense and recommended I hire an attorney. I thought the whole thing was ridiculous, and I didn't hire an attorney. Candy and I went to court on the appointed date, but Harry did not show up. The hearing was rescheduled, and we went a second time. Once again, Harry didn't show up. It was scheduled for a third time, and once again Harry didn't show up. This time, the city attorney recommended to the judge that the case be dropped. I remember the judge saying, "Well, I don't know if I can do that," but he did. Several weeks later when Harry saw me out in my yard, he came over and apologized to me.

In about this same time period, I was beginning to have a lot of doubts about the Catholic Church. I had been reading the Bible some, and it really caused me to question a lot of what I was taught in Catholicism. I signed up for and attended a Catholic conversion class. I thought that would be a good place to get a lot of my questions answered. What I discovered was that most of my questions concerning Catholicism just couldn't be answered, at least not my satisfaction. I learned that a great deal of what I had been taught as a Catholic was not biblical at all, but we still continued attending the Catholic Church for a while longer.

A Season of Sin

The following is an account of an episode in my life that nearly caused my demise. I believe it was in the early '80s that it all began. It is now 2001, so it will be by the grace of God that I recall the most important details.

I would have been in my early thirties. I had been married for about ten years, and my wife at that time and I had three sons. At age three, our firstborn son was diagnosed with cancer. He had been on and off chemotherapy for nearly six years.

One evening, my wife was reading the local newspaper and came across an ad for hypnotherapy. She apparently thought I was overly shy. However, I didn't consider myself to be an introvert or an extrovert but somewhere in the middle. She suggested to me that I go see this hypnotist as a means of overcoming my shyness. It sounded like a good idea to me. I had the idea that I would be hypnotized once. I assumed that he would hypnotize me, tell me that I was an outgoing, fearless extrovert or whatever, and I would be a changed person. I was excited about the whole idea, so I telephoned his office and made an appointment.

At my appointment time, Mr. Doug Settles spoke with me and informed me that he was a psychologist who specialized in hypnotherapy. He gave me a list of questions to answer. Based on the questions and the way I answered them, he determined that I was a victim of childhood sexual abuse. He suggested to me that I was fearful of mankind because of that sexual abuse.

To overcome that fear and become the person I was really meant to be, I would have to relive each episode of sexual abuse through hypnotic regressions. He told me that to relive these incidents of sexual abuse through hypnosis would be very painful. I would not just remember them, he said, but I would actually relive them through hypnosis. He told me the pain would be more real and intense than it was during the actual event. I was told to try and remember the worst pain I had ever experienced and multiply it by a hundred. "That," he said, "will be close to the pain you will experience."

I had no memory of sexual abuse, but I knew that my sisters had been sexually abused by my dad. Although I had no memory of any abuse to me, since I knew there had been sexual abuse in my family, I agreed to do the hypnotic regressions. Mr. Settles wanted to spend the last fifteen minutes of my appointment time doing a hypnotic relaxation technique with me. I was sitting in a very comfortable large reclined easy chair. He told me to raise my left arm. He then told me to slowly lower my raised arm. As I did so, he told me I was going deeper and deeper into a state of relaxation. I felt as though I was falling, but it was a very pleasant feeling, something I had never experienced before.I truly was more relaxed than ever before, and I wondered how these mere words coming from his mouth could be so powerful and cause me to have such a pleasant, wonderful feeling. Before I left his office, we scheduled an appointment for the following week, at which time, we were going to attempt to have me, via hypnosis, regress to the first incident of sexual abuse. I felt excited but somewhat nervous about my second appointment. I certainly did not want to experience the pain, but I looked forward to the new person I was going to be.

Mr. Settles had me sit in the comfortable chair as on my first visit.I don't recall the exact words he spoke to me, but nothing happened this time. I didn't have a regression, nor did I recall anything, but I told him I thought it was kind of chilly in the room. He told me the temperature was fine, that it was about seventy degrees, but I was doing what he called *blocking* or refusing to remember that I was feeling cold. He said it was because I was "blocking" that I was not able to have a regression. We decided to try again the next week. During the remaining appointment time, Mr. Settles began to teach me the technique of self-hypnosis. Mr. Settles tried to cause me to have a hypnotic regression. We had no success, and he insisted that I was continuing to *block*. I was beginning to get discouraged, but by this time, I was beginning to master the technique of self-hypnosis. This was an encouragement to me.

I practiced self-hypnosis every evening. I would lie on my bed, and starting with my toes and working my way up to my scalp, I would tell myself that every muscle and nerve in my entire body was completely, totally relaxed. I imagined that I was very heavy, as if made of concrete, and that I was sinking into the bed. It was a very pleasant feeling. My arms would feel numb, as if the circulation of blood had been cut off, but without the unpleasant tingling sensation that occurs when circulation really is cut off.

After a while the word *heavy* became my key word. I would lie down and say to myself, "My arms are heavy," and almost immediately, I would be in this very relaxed mode. I became so good at this that I eventually did not even have to lie down. Even while standing, I could just think the word *heavy*, and I would soon be in this relaxed mode. I felt like I was really accomplishing something. I knew how to do something that few other people knew how to do. Most people had no idea what it meant to be really relaxed.

When I explained to Mr. Settles what I had accomplished, he was impressed. He said I was at the first level of hypnosis every time my arms and hands had that pleasant, numb feeling. "This," he said, "is the level of hypnosis in which most of the work is done."

It appeared that it was useless for him to try to get me to have a regression, so he told me to continue with my daily self-hypnosis. He told me that once I was in that relaxed level, I should suggest to myself that I have a regression back to my first incident of sexual abuse. He warned me, however, that before I make that suggestion to myself, I first should imagine myself being surrounded by bright light. "The bright light," he explained, "is to protect you from evil spirits that might try to interfere." He explained to me that there are different levels or planes that can be reached via hypnosis and that there is a particular plane in which evil spirits dwell. He said that if I should reach that plane, I would need the protection of the bright light.

I practiced daily but without success. I was becoming very discouraged. Since the hypnotic regressions were not happening, Mr. Settles suggested I try dream therapy. I kept a spiral notebook with an ink pen in the spiral under my pillow. Every evening before I went to sleep, I would hypnotize myself and say to myself that I would dream in vivid detail. When the dream was complete, I would remember it in vivid detail and immediately record it in the notebook.

To my amazement, and perhaps your disbelief, it worked. Upon completion of a dream, while I was still asleep, I would take the notebook from under my pillow and record the dream. I would then put the notebook back under my pillow. When I awoke in the morning, I did not know whether or not I had recorded a dream until I looked at the notebook. The writing was anything but neat and did not follow the lines on the paper. I was able to read it, though, and remember the dream. I would then rewrite the dream so it was legible.

As I recall, I recorded a dream almost every night. Every week when I went to see Mr. Settles, I would present him with what I had written. He would then spend the first half hour or so of each session reading what I had written. I continued this dream procedure and my sessions with Mr. Settles for at least a year. Not only did I meet with him privately every week, but sometimes in the evening, there would be a group meeting and discussion. At these group sessions, people who had hypnotic regressions would share some of their experiences. Most of the stories I heard were horrifying, and I found most of them difficult to believe. Nevertheless, I was jealous because they were having regressions, and I was not.

At one of the group sessions, a few of us were just visiting with Mr. Settles. We were talking about hypnosis. There were four of us sitting with him. We were just playing around, but at some point, he told us to close our eyes. He then told us our eyelids were very heavy, and we could not open our eyes. I tried with all my might, as did the other three, but we were not able to open our eyes until he told us we could. We all thought it was funny.

Although I became an expert at the act of self-hypnosis, I do not claim to be an expert on the subject. I am sure we can all understand how making suggestions to ourselves can change our behavior, but how is it possible that the words from someone else's mouth can have so much power over us? This I do not know.

At each of my future sessions with Mr. Settles, he would read my written dreams in total awe and amazement. He would try to analyze the dreams for me. In every instance, he was able to make some connection between my dreams and childhood sexual abuse. In some of my dreams, I would be flying. That was an indication to Mr. Settles that while I was being abused, I would become someone with superpowers and was able to fly in order to escape the pain. The dreams I recorded were indeed horror stories. To say that they were bizarre would be an understatement. Mr. Settles told me he had never seen or heard of anyone who had dreams such as mine and was able to record them as I did. I was paying him to sit there and enjoy reading what I had written, and it was beginning to make me angry. His enjoyment from reading my dreams was doing me no good whatsoever.

There were two other hypnotherapists who shared Mr. Settles's office, and all were of the same school of thought. They believed each of us has a spirit guide. They believed in reincarnation and that it was possible, through hypnosis, to communicate with other living persons who were not then present, as well as with the dead.

On one occasion, Mr. Settles told me he had communicated with my son who had cancer. He believed that infants in their mother's womb can know what the mother is thinking. He told me that my son learned from his mother, my wife, that she was very unhappy in our marriage. She wanted to divorce me, but because she was pregnant, she could not do so. According to Mr. Settles, out of love for his mother, my son decided to die so his mother could divorce me and be happy. I actually believed that lie. It was not until my son was three years of age that he was diagnosed with cancer.

On another occasion while I was in his office, Mr. Settles asked me if I wanted to try to contact my son. I said I did, and we each entered a state of hypnosis. I heard absolutely nothing. Mr. Settles told me he did hear from my son, but the message came so quickly that he couldn't tell what it was. He said it was very clear, though, that my son did not want to communicate with me. Hearing that news only added to my discouragement and depression.

Mr. Settles told me he was one of the few therapists who kept a Bible on his shelf. For some reason, I was impressed by that. At that time, I had never read the Bible. I was of the Catholic persuasion and had a heart for the Lord even as a child. Mr. Settles told me he thought the Bible was in great error. I had no reason not to believe him, but even so, from the beginning and throughout all my time and experience with Mr. Settles, I continued to pray to God.

Mr. Settles said he believed in reincarnation and that each of us had to keep coming back until we got it right. He believed Jesus was the first of God's creations to get it right and to not have to come back again. He believed God created us by dividing Himself into parts. This would, of course, mean there was no such thing or place as hell. According to this false belief, everyone would eventually return to God, and He (God) would be complete again. It was easy and desirable to believe there was no hell.

As time went on, I became more and more depressed. I continued, in vain, to try to have regressions back to my childhood abuse, but I just wasn't able to do so. My wife, three sons, and I lived in a very nice new house that we had built. I decided that my family was interfering with my success. I needed more quiet and time alone, so I bought another house and moved out. The house I bought was a roach-infested place on the poor side of town. It wasn't pleasant, but I was sure I would now be able to have the necessary regressions to get my life straightened out.

I still saw my sons on a regular basis. They would often come over and spend the weekend with me. They wanted to be with their dad, but they preferred living in the much-nicer house, which they were used to.

After about six months, I still had not had a regression. I was beginning to lose all hope. One evening, I just decided to go back home. My wife was not happy that I had left, and she did not welcome me back. I was beginning to think death was the only answer. Some of us who were seeing Mr. Settles thought it odd that every person who ever went to see him was determined by him to be a victim of childhood sexual abuse. He assured us that our spirit guides had directed us to him. I continued to pray. Sometimes the only words I could utter were, "Lord, help me."

On one occasion, I received a letter from a lady I had dated in high school. She said she had become a born-again Christian and was praying for my salvation. I thought that rather odd because while we were dating, I was a devout Catholic, and she seemed to have no faith at all. Along with her letter, she sent a small Bible.

Some days later, I picked up the Bible. I didn't really believe it was true, and I did not plan on reading it. I opened it, however, and began to read a passage of scripture in which we were being told to stay away from certain things. Included in that list was hypnosis. I really didn't think much of it and threw the Bible back down on my desk. I continued to ask God to help me, but I also continued the practice of self-hypnosis.

A week or so later, I picked up a different Bible. I remember this one had a green cover. I think it was given to me by the Gideons one day as I was entering a building. Once again, I picked up this different Bible with no intention of reading it. This time when I opened the Bible, I once again saw the same list of things God's people were supposed to stay away from. I clearly saw the word *hypnosis*. Again, I gave it no thought and continued with self-hypnosis.

It had been at least a year now since I had first seen Mr. Settles. I had lost all hope. I knew I would never be the person I meant to be, and I felt useless. I didn't really want to die but saw no way out of the mess I was in.

It was on a Saturday that I decided to end my life. I went into the garage. There were three entrances, and I made sure each was unlocked. I made a lot of noise so my wife would hear me. I then got into my truck and started the engine. My wife heard me, and she knew what was happening. She probably assumed the doors were locked, and she ran to our neighbors to get help. My neighbor was soon there and easily flung open the overhead door. There I was, sad, pitiful, and embarrassed. My neighbors stood there looking at me, not knowing what to say or do.

I slammed the truck into reverse and went screeching out of the driveway. I drove for a couple of hours. I remember screaming at God that I hated him. I eventually calmed down and returned home. I think the whole purpose of that stunt was to see if anyone really cared about me.

A few days later, I came across a third Bible. I'm sure you can guess what happened. With this third Bible, I again opened to the same scripture and clearly saw the word *hypnosis*. This time, it clicked. I finally saw the light. God had been hearing my cry for help, but I had not been listening to His answer. Now I knew I had to forget about hypnosis and regressions.

What I am going to say now is probably the most important part of this writing. Although the main subject matter of this writing has been hypnosis and my sin of continuing to practice it, I think the more important matter is that of God's love for us. It was not by chance or coincidence that I opened three different Bibles and saw the word *hypnosis* and the warning to stay away from it.

Years ago, I told the story of the Bible to the pastor of our church. He then began to scratch his head and tried to recall which Bible translation used the word *hypnosis*. He did not understand. I pray you will. The particular translation of any of the three Bibles I looked at is entirely irrelevant. What I am saying here is that it was a miracle. Had any of you been there and been looking over my shoulder at the scripture I was reading, you probably would not have seen the word *hypnosis*. It was the only word that I could have seen that would have gotten my attention at all. Even then, I had to see it three times before the light came on.

Suppose one of the three translations did actually use the word hypnosis. What is the likelihood that each of the three Bibles given to me by three different people would have all been the same translation, using the word *hypnosis*? If that were true, that also would have been miraculous.

After deciding to heed God's warning and stay away from hypnosis, I telephoned the former high school girlfriend and told my story. She gave me the phone number of the lady who had led her to the Lord. I went to this lady's house and talked with her and her husband. I told them I had repented of practicing hypnosis.

She then asked me if I wanted to pray and receive the Holy Spirit. She told me I would feel a warm sensation in the center of my stomach, and I would then be able to pray in a different language. Because of what I had been through during the past year, I found that difficult to believe. She began to pray in the Spirit. That was a totally new experience for me. I had never heard such a thing, and it sounded like gibberish to me.

I believed I had nothing to lose, so I repeated the (English) words she asked me to pray. I was sincere but doubtful. But to my amazement, it happened just as she said it would. I did have a pleasant sensation in my stomach. I had a desire to speak this new language. I was embarrassed, so I only uttered a few words of this new language. There was nothing magical or overpowering. I had the desire to pray in this new language, but I had to make the decision to do so.

As I was driving home, I prayed in this new language. I was amazed at how easily the words came, how they flowed so easily. I had no idea what the words meant, but as I continued to pray, tears of joy began to run down my cheeks. For the first time in over a year, I saw hope. My life had changed in just that one evening.

I had saved all the writings of the dreams I had experienced in the previous year. If the writings had all been bound together, it would have been a thick book, a book I am sure would have made the bestseller list. So where did these dreams come from? Certainly not from God. I believe I had opened myself up to demonic influence, and the dreams were given to me by demonic spirits. In a hundred years, I would never have been able to think up or write anything even close to what I wrote while practicing self-hypnosis. Because I repented of that practice, I destroyed all the written dreams. I have read the Bible from cover to cover, and although I don't understand all that I have read, I believe the Bible is the Word of God and is without error.

Some of you older folks may remember Jean Dixon. Years ago, there were many news articles (mostly in the tabloids) about her and her predictions of the future. Mr. Doug Settles told me she was correct in most of her predictions, and she received her information while in a hypnotic trance. Hypnosis is not make-believe but very real and very serious.

Deuteronomy 13:1–3 says,

> If a prophet, or one who foretells by dreams, appears among you and announces a miraculous sign or wonder, and if the sign or wonder of which he has spoken takes place and he says, "Let us follow other gods" (gods you have not known)

"and let us worship them," you must not listen to the words of that prophet or dreamer.

Acts 16:16 of the Bible says,

> Once when we were going to a place of prayer, we were met by a slave girl who had a spirit by which she predicted the future. She earned a great deal of money for her owners by fortune-telling.

In regard to reincarnation, the Bible says in Hebrews 9:27–28,

> Just as man is destined to die once, and after that to face judgment, so Christ was sacrificed once to take away the sins of many people; and he will appear a second time, not to bear sin, but to bring salvation to those who are waiting for him.

Hypnosis is used today for various reasons. Some want to see a change in behavior, such as to stop smoking cigarettes or to lose weight. Some medical doctors use hypnosis as a means of controlling pain. There is no doubt hypnosis is a powerful tool. Perhaps if Adam had not sinned and Satan had not entered the scene, hypnosis would be a good thing. However, that is not the case. Even Mr. Doug Settles and others in his league who do not accept the Bible as God's Word recognize the danger of practicing hypnosis. Therefore, they teach the idea of surrounding oneself with bright light as protection from evil spirits while in a state of hypnosis.

During the year I was seeing and being counseled by Mr. Settles, I met many people who had been seeing him much longer. Some of these people claimed to be having regressions back to childhood as well as back to past lives. However, I never knew of anyone who had completed hypnotherapy with Mr. Settles and was well. No one was being cured.

I believe I was a victim of childhood sexual abuse only to the extent that I was living in a household where it was taking place and was aware of it. My eldest sister was sexually abused as a child, and she was and still is today what I would consider to be an extrovert. She did well in school and was outgoing and popular.

If anyone reading this is a victim of sexual or any other type of abuse, only you can decide whether or not you want to seek counseling. It is not too late at any age. My recommendation, of course, would be Christian, biblical counseling. One thing is certain: Whether you, as a victim, seek counseling or not, you must forgive the person who abused you.

Hypnosis is indeed a powerful tool. Among many biblical scholars, it falls into the category of witchcraft. Although it is a powerful tool, it does not even begin to come close to the power of prayer. Hypnosis is defined as an artificially induced state resembling sleep characterized by heightened susceptibility to suggestion. In addition, to hypnotize is defined as the ability to influence, control, or direct completely, as if by hypnotic suggestion, as well as to put or be able to put others into a hypnotic state.

A few months ago, my dad passed away. He was the one, of course, who was abusing my sisters. One of my Christian sisters and I had been praying for his salvation for many years. Just about a year ago, he prayed the Sinner's prayer with my sister who had been praying for him. He accepted Jesus as his Savior. I do believe he is with our Lord now.

A New Church

Shortly after recovering from my episode with hypnosis and all that was related to it, Candy and I began attending Living Stones Christian Church. That was the church my high school girlfriend had been attending, and I wanted to check it out. I first attended by myself. Candy was reluctant to leave the Catholic Church, and it took some persuading on my part to get her to visit Living Stones Church. Living Stones Church was a Bible-believing, nondenominational church.

My first visit to Living Stones Church was a totally new experience for me. I had never attended any church service except Catholic. Living Stones Church had a small congregation, but the people there appeared to be genuine. During worship, they all sang loudly, many raised their hands in praise to God, and some even danced for joy. I witnessed some people with tears running down their cheeks.

At first, I wondered what I was doing there. I felt out of place and actually felt a little guilty about not being at the Catholic Mass on a Sunday. I knew I was attending a Christian church service, but because of many years of Catholic teaching, I wondered if perhaps I was committing a sin by purposefully missing Catholic Mass. I did get over that false belief, and I soon learned that everything being done at Living Stones Church in regard to worship was biblical.

There is much scripture concerning the worshiping of our Lord. We are told in scripture to praise God with song and musical instruments. We are told to lift our hands, which is symbolic of reaching out to receive God. And we are also told to clap our hands and dance before the Lord. I even learned that the name Living Stones, which I thought was odd, was from the Bible.

It took me a while to get up the nerve to worship in some of these ways that were new to me, but once I did, it proved to be a truly wonderful experience. Candy and our sons did finally start attending Living Stones Church with me. Candy was never comfortable there and never did really break away from Catholicism.

One day while I was working at the contact lens lab, I received an unexpected phone call. It was from an employment agency that specializes in the optical field. They did not know me. Their technique for recruiting people was to simply telephone optical manufacturing companies and ask to speak with the manager. In this case, it turned out to be me.

I was asked if I would be interested in interviewing for a contact lens managerial position in Maryland. I saw nothing to lose and said I would. I did not have any plans of leaving Precision Optics Inc., but business was slow, and I did have some concerns about my future there. One of my sisters and her family were living in Waldorf, Maryland, so that was encouraging. I also thought that it might help our marriage if we got away from Council Bluffs, Iowa, and all family influence.

Within two weeks, Candy and I were on a plane headed for Washington, DC. My sister Linda met us at the airport and drove me to the Marriott Hotel in Gaithersburg, Maryland. I met Dr. John Javier there, and he drove me to the contact lens lab that was still being built. We met another man there, and the two of them began bombarding me with questions. After about two hours, Dr. Javier drove me back to the Marriott, where Candy and my sister were waiting for me. They had had fun shopping, and I was thinking that the job interview had gone well.

About two weeks had passed when I received a phone call from Dr. Javier. He told me I was the person they were looking for, and they wanted me to start in about a month. He thought the new contact lens lab would be finished by then. They were going to start me out at $4,000 more per year than I was earning at Precision Optics Inc. That sounded pretty good to me, and I accepted his offer. When I gave a two-week notice to Mr. Woodford at Precision Optics, he became very upset. He said, "What am I going to do for a manager?"

He told me he would give me a nice increase in pay if I stayed. I was flattered but declined to accept his offer. So after twelve years with Precision Optics Inc., Mr. Woodford didn't even let me finish my two weeks. I went home and now had a month of free time before leaving for Maryland.

The thought of packing up and moving my family to Maryland was pretty frightening for me. I wasn't even sure I would be able to handle the job, but I was determined that moving away would help my marriage.

The actual company that I would be working for was Southern Optical Company Inc., and they were located in North Carolina. They were a very large corporation with thirteen optical manufacturing sites. Dr. John Javier was an ophthalmologist and started Southern's first contact lens facility at the North Carolina location. He believed the Washington, DC, area would be an ideal location for a second contact lens lab and persuaded the owner of Southern Optical to let him start one there. Gaithersburg, Maryland, turned out to be the actual location.

This was going to be a huge responsibility for me. My immediate supervisor would be in North Carolina, so I was really going to be on my own to make this thing work. I flew to Maryland while my family stayed in Iowa. When I arrived there, the contact lens lab was not yet completed, so I did not have a great deal to do. I got in touch with a realtor and began looking for a house for us to buy. Our house in Iowa was not sold yet, but we did have it on the market. I found us a new house in Damascus, Maryland. It wasn't quite as nice as the one we were leaving behind in Iowa. It was October now, and the house would not be completed until the end of November.

Southern Optical had given me a car to drive and a sum of money to stay in a motel until I had a house bought. Simple math revealed to me that the money they had given me was going to be gone before I was able to move into the house. It was now November. I decided to fly back home to Iowa for Thanksgiving and then drive back to Maryland with my family.

Candy and I had already made plans with Bekins Moving Company. They could come and pack up our belongings at any time. The driver of the tractor trailer decided to come on the day after Thanksgiving. It just so happened that we were experiencing a pretty bad blizzard on that day. I didn't really care, though. I was eager to get on the road back to Maryland and begin our new adventure.

Near the end of the day, most of our belongings were on the tractor trailer, including my pickup truck. Interstate 80 was packed with snow and was officially closed. I decided we would drive anyway. The going was very slow at first, but after a hundred miles or so, the road became clear, and we made pretty good time. The total trip took us about two and a half days. The actual driving time was about twenty-one hours. I swore I'd never make the trip by car again. When we arrived in Maryland, our house was not yet ready for us. Candy dropped me off at the contact lens lab, and she and our sons drove on to Waldorf, Maryland, to stay with my sister until our house was completed. By now, I had a few employees and was beginning to get them trained. Starting a contact lens lab from scratch proved to be very challenging. It was very lonely being in a new town and not knowing even one person. It was so nice to have someone to talk with. I was really eager to hire and train more people.

I didn't have any money left, so I was actually living in the contact lens lab. I kept a suitcase with my belongings in my office, and I kept a sleeping bag in one of the empty cabinets. In the morning, I'd get up early, wash my hair, and shave in the men's room. I'd then go out and start the car to melt the frost off the windows. No one ever suspected I was living in the lab. It was extremely boring, to say the least. I did call Waldorf and visit with my family in the evenings. I accepted the position with Southern Optical on the condition that I would not have to do any selling. Selling just was not my forte. Dr. Javier had hired someone else in the DC area to do all the selling. I had plenty to do, though. I was responsible for training and hiring all contact lens technicians. There were no other contact lens manufacturing labs in the area, so there was no chance of hiring someone with even a little experience. I was responsible for purchasing all the equipment and supplies and to keep everything in good working order. I was also the timekeeper, disciplinarian, and counselor to all the employees. It was a slow start, but we were finally up and running. I had taught each employee how to perform one phase of the operation, and we were now manufacturing excellent-quality contact lenses. The salesman was doing his job, and local eye doctors were beginning to call in lens orders.

In about two weeks, our house was ready, and we moved in. The moving company had arrived before the house was completed, so they had to leave all our belongings packed up and stored in the basement. We didn't have much help because we didn't know anyone in the area yet, but we did okay.

One day, I was visiting with one of the plumbers working to get the contact lens lab ready. I told him that I was looking for a church to attend in the Damascus area. He said he was Catholic, but he had a friend attending a nondenominational church in Damascus. The next Sunday, I visited the Household of Faith Church. The congregation was larger than that of Living Stones Church, but other than that, it was very similar. Once my family and I were settled into our new house, we all began attending the Household of Faith Church.

A long time before my family had moved to Maryland, Mike had been diagnosed with sarcoma (bone cancer). They first talked of removing one of Mike's arms but then later decided the cancer had already metastasized. Mike went through another season of chemotherapy and seemed to be doing well. By the time we were ready to leave Iowa for Maryland, we were sure Mike was doing fine. We had only been in Maryland for a few months when we noticed a lump on one of Mike's arms. Mike had just turned twelve. For eight years, he had been in and out of hospitals. Sometimes the chemotherapy seemed to be worse than the disease. I really did not want Mike to go through it again.

We had always prayed that Mike would be healed, but at the same time, we had him go through more chemotherapy. I made the decision that he would have no more chemotherapy. We were going to pray and trust God to heal Mike. The tumor on Mike's arm continued to grow. Candy insisted that we take him for treatment, but I stood firm in believing Mike would be healed.

One day, Candy invited Roger Melson to our house. Roger was the pastor at Household of Faith Church. On Candy's behalf, he tried to persuade me to let her take Mike for treatment. I thought he was lacking in faith, and I asked him to leave my house.

After a period of time, I did finally concede to let Candy take Mike to be seen by a doctor. I was really concerned about Mike and was questioning whether or not I had made the right decision. My hands were really full trying to keep the new contact lens lab going. Candy was left with the responsibility of getting Mike the medical care he needed. Mike was seriously ill.

The doctor tried to get him admitted into the National Institutes of Health in Bethesda, Maryland. They would not accept Mike because they were not doing a study at that time on the particular type of cancer Mike had. They basically told us to take Mike home and make him as comfortable as possible and let him die. Even today, I often refer to the National Institutes of Health as the "Hospital of Political Medicine."

I was so busy with the contact lens lab that I never even had the opportunity to meet this particular doctor. He did seem to really care. He suggested to Candy that she leave his name out of it but call our representative in congress and try to get Mike into the National Institutes of Health. The pressure of congress did help, and the hospital finally agreed to treat Mike. They agreed to give Mike chemotherapy, but they would not admit him into the hospital as a patient. Candy had to drive Mike from Damascus to Bethesda on a daily basis so he could get chemotherapy. Mike was really too sick now to be making this daily trip. Chemotherapy always made Mike very sick to his stomach and caused him to be very weak. Of course, he lost his hair every time he had treatment. The chemotherapy always seemed to work, though. The cancer would stop growing, and Mike would be in remission.

One day when Candy was arriving home from the hospital with Mike, I was already home from work. Mike was walking up to our front door when he tripped and fell. He was not injured, but seeing him so frail and then watching him fall made me so angry. I was angry at God for allowing my son to suffer so. We had a large painting of a depiction of Christ hanging on one of our walls. I took it down and threw it on the floor as hard as I could. A corner of the painting was badly damaged. I hung the painting back on the wall, but several months later, I took it down and threw it in the trash, not because I was angry at God but because I decided I didn't want any false images of Christ in my house.

In all Mike's suffering, he never complained. I think he knew he may die, and he was more concerned about his mother and me. He only listened to Christian worship and praise music. He wanted to have someone pray with him, and I sometimes felt guilty because I didn't want to pray as long as Mike did.

We had been living in Maryland for just a few months when the Lord gave me the following dream.

Testimony
Dream of March 23, 1984

In my dream, I was sitting on a long wooden seat, like a pew or the seats in a train station. It seemed somewhat like it was in a train station, but there were no people around, except for one other. I was dressed as I usually am, very casual. I was wearing blue jeans.

I was sitting in about the middle of the long seat. Down at the right end of the seat was a man kneeling on the floor. His elbows rested on the wooden seat, and his hands supported his bowed head. I knew he was praying. He had long hair, and he was dressed as they dressed back in the time when Jesus was on earth.

As I sat there, it occurred to me that it was Jesus. I knew it was Jesus, but I just sat there, not doing or saying anything. Then I became so very aware that it was Jesus. I knew I had to do something. I slid down the seat and placed my hand on His shoulder. He looked up at me, and His face was so filled with love and compassion. There are no words in my vocabulary to describe how He looked. I had never seen such a look on the face of any man on earth. I cried out to Him, "Jesus, I love you."

He reached out his arms, and we hugged each other. I had never felt so comforted or felt so much love. I told Him I was so very glad to be with Him, and He told me that He was glad to be with me. He seemed to be filled with great joy, as I was, over our being together.

I then tried to argue with Jesus. I wanted to explain to Him that He was confused. I was saying, "Jesus, You don't understand. You shouldn't be filled with joy over being with me. I'm just me. I'm just a person. You're God. I'm supposed to be filled with joy over being with You. You've got it all wrong. You should not be filled with joy over being with me."

At that time, my twelve-year-old son had been ill with cancer for nine years. I wanted to believe that this dream somehow meant that my son would be healed, but there was no evidence that he was being healed. The chemotherapy was no longer working, but I refused to believe that my son would die.

Mike's Death

October 19, 1984
Seven Months Following Dream

On this morning, my in-laws were visiting from Iowa. I took the day off work to take my in-laws sightseeing in Washington, DC. Candy and her grandmother were going to take our son Michael to the hospital for his regular treatment of chemotherapy. At this time, Mike was very, very ill and extremely weak. He could not walk. Although he was twelve years old, we had to pick him up and carry him.

Mike wanted to take a bath before going to the hospital. It somehow became my responsibility to bathe Mike that morning. I could not recall that in twelve years, I had ever bathed Mike. Even when he was a young child or baby, I never bathed him. I guess I just thought it was his mother's job, and I never did it. But on this occasion, I carefully picked Mike up and carried him into the bathroom. I helped him undress, and I lifted him into the tub of water I had already run.

As I helped him to bathe, it was the first time I had really looked at his body. As I ran the washcloth over his body, I could see and count every bone. There was very little flesh remaining. He was so very ill, and yet I refused to believe that he might die.

After bathing Mike, I headed for DC with my in-laws, while Mike's mother and grandmother took him to the National Institutes of Health in Bethesda, Maryland. When my in-laws and I arrived back home that evening, there was a note on the front door of the house. I was to telephone the hospital immediately. I ran to the phone and did so. Mike's grandmother answered the phone in his hospital room. She informed me that Mike had died that day. It was, of course, very painful and shocking to hear this news.

Sometime later, I recalled the dream and tried to understand why my son died when I was so sure he was going to live. Six years later, I still recall the dream. I believe the dream did, in fact, have to do with the death of my son and my ability or inability to deal with it.

The moment of happiness, of joy that I had with Jesus, I cannot forget. It pains me that I can't recall that moment in more detail. I have the great joy, however, of knowing that my son is with our Lord, experiencing the joy that I felt for just a moment. He is experiencing the love and companionship of Jesus every day. Knowing that brings me a great peace. I recalled that on the night Mike died, I would not have called him back, even if I had the power to do so. I would not have called him back from that joy.

I believe it was God's plan that I not be at the hospital the day Mike died. Everything happened according to God's plan. I bathed my son for the first time ever. Although I didn't know it at the time, I believe I was, in essence, helping to prepare my son for burial by bathing him as I did. I believe God kept me away from the hospital that day because he knew I would not have been able to cope with standing there watching my son slowly pass away. I didn't have the strength for that, so the Lord kept me from it.

I think the main purpose of the dream having been given to me was so I would have the peace of knowing that my son is, in fact, with Jesus and experiencing great joy and happiness. In the dream, it seemed to me as if I was in a train station. I think that is significant in that we are on a journey. It was also significant that in the dream, I saw myself as being dressed very casually, as I usually wear blue jeans. It didn't matter to Jesus. He accepted me as I was. He loves and accepts us just as we are.

In the dream, I knew Jesus was praying. I believe now, He was praying for me. I believe He was praying to the Father for me that I would recognize Him and go to Him. That prayer was answered when I slid down the seat and placed my hand on the shoulder of Jesus. There was great joy for both of us.

Jesus was filled with great joy over being with me. You'd think I was somebody really special that Jesus would be so filled with joy over being with me. You know what? I am. It took me a long time to realize and understand that, but to Jesus, I am somebody really special. We all are. I believe that when Jesus was hanging on the cross, He saw each one of us individually. And I believe he was saying, even though I was not yet born, "Larry, I do this for you because I love you. John, Steve, Mary, etc. I do this for you."

I have only recently become aware of how personal our relationship with Jesus is. We were in a large train station, yet it was just Jesus and I, one on one, no distractions, no other people around. As is only possible with God, when each of us talks with Him, we have His full, undivided attention.

On the evening Mike died, I took our two younger sons down to Mike's room. I told them that Mike had gone to heaven to be with Jesus, so we would not be seeing him anymore. Tim, who was only about five years of age, said, "Did Mike die?"

I said, "Yes, honey, he did."

Tim then said, "That makes me sad."

I agreed with him that we were all very sad and would miss Mike very much. I told him that Mike wasn't sick anymore, and that he was very happy now. Later on that evening, both Tim and Steve, at separate times, went down to spend some time alone in Mike's room.

We had funeral services at Molesworth Funeral Home in Damascus, but Candy wanted the actual burial to be in Iowa.

I received my Maryland driver's license during my first month in Maryland. Candy never bothered to get a Maryland license at all. Now that she was wanting Mike to be buried in Iowa, it really made me wonder what her intentions were.

When we were talking with the funeral director at Molesworth Funeral Home, he used the terminology *remains* when he referred to Mike. At first, I took offense, but then it occurred to me that he was absolutely correct. Mike wasn't there anymore. He was in heaven, and it was just his remains we were dealing with.

We made arrangements to fly back to Iowa, but Mike's remains had to be flown back on a separate airline. We were told that some airline passengers might get upset if they knew there was a corpse on board the plane. Therefore, some airlines, like the one we were flying on, refused to transport a corpse. I thought the whole idea was absurd, but there was nothing we could do about it.

In the evening we were having visitation at Molesworth Funeral Home, some people commented on how strong I was. "As strong as a rock," one person said.

I was not strong, though. At that point, I hadn't even looked at Mike in the casket. I didn't even want to go into that particular room. I finally did because I knew I had to. I had to see Mike's remains in the coffin and accept the fact that he had really died. I kept control of my emotions and cried in private.

Mike's remains were buried at Saint Joseph Cemetery in Council Bluffs, Iowa. Trying to describe what it is like to lose a child isn't even possible because there is nothing to compare it to.

As we were flying back to Maryland, I could only wonder what the future held for us. When we were back in our house, it was difficult for me to go into what had been Mike's room. It was difficult to hold his shoes and know that he would never wear them again. I was truly happy for Mike that he was in heaven, and his suffering was over, but knowing that didn't minimize the feeling of his loss to us.

I'm not sure what Candy did to deal with the pain. I buried myself in work. I returned to my job right away and kept as busy as I could. I had read once that when a child dies, one parent usually blames the other. I hadn't thought of or considered that until I saw it happen. I knew our lives would be changed, but I was totally unprepared for what happened.

I knew that Candy had never really wanted to move to Maryland. I think she was trying really hard to do what she had believed was right. She moved to Maryland even though she didn't really want to. I respected her for doing so, and I thought she must care about our marriage. Our relationship had been troubled, but it would soon get much worse.

As it turned out, Candy did blame me for Mike's death. She believed that if I had not made them move to Maryland, Mike would have been all right. I'm sure the move from Iowa to Maryland had nothing to do with Mike's death. The fact that I refused to let Mike receive chemotherapy right from the start probably did. I think from Candy's point of view, it was no different than if I had deliberately killed Mike. Her anger toward me was nearly unbearable to me. I really didn't understand what was happening.

Unfortunately, even though I was Christian, I didn't return a blessing for anger. I returned anger for anger. This book is about me, so I won't go into detail about Candy's behavior, except to mention one thing. Because of her anger toward me, she discontinued washing my clothes. Many more things happened throughout the course of the year. My response to Candy's actions toward me was not good. Before we had even left Iowa, Candy had been somewhat conditioned by her family. They did not want her to leave Iowa. I heard her dad tell her many times, "You won't like it out there."

After Mike's death, it appeared to me that Candy was deliberately trying to provoke me to anger. I think she was looking for a way to justify going back to Iowa. Candy and I were so angry with each other that we could hardly stand one another. We went to see Roger Melson, the pastor of Household of Faith, for counseling. Roger was a decent man, and he truly loved the Lord, but he was not able to help us.

Our situation only continued to get worse. Sometimes I would be so angry at Candy, I would tell her to leave. Although I never did any physical harm to Candy, on more than one occasion, I threatened to kill her if she did not leave. As ridiculous as it probably sounds, that isn't what I wanted at all. It reminds me of someone who tries to commit suicide. In most cases, they don't really want to die. It's just a cry for help. It's a stupid thing to do, but when a person is at the end of his rope, he'll do stupid things. I know because I did. Candy and I were both at the end of our rope. We knew we couldn't continue like we were. I didn't have an answer. Candy's answer was to leave.

It was October. It had been a year to the month since Mike had died. As I was approaching our house after a day at work, I felt an eerie feeling, and I knew something was wrong. As I pulled into our driveway, I saw tire marks in the grass. I became nauseated and feared going into the house. I sat in the car for a few minutes and then went and opened the front door. The house was empty! There was some furniture remaining, but my family was gone.

I truly felt ill. I had to decide what to do. I started making phone calls, but no one knew anything. My next-door neighbor said she saw the U-Haul trailer at the house and thought about giving me a call at work, but then she decided I probably knew what was going on and decided not to call me.

After the way I treated Candy and threatened her, I should not have been surprised that she was gone. Now, not only was I surprised, but I was frantic. At this point, I didn't even consider that she may have gone back to Iowa. I continued telephoning people and began to drive around and search. I thought maybe she was staying with a lady she had befriended at Household of Faith Church. I telephoned that lady, and she denied that Candy was there.

Harry Down lived about a block away. He was a mutual friend of both Candy and myself. I telephoned him and told him what had happened. He was angry and could hardly believe Candy would have done such a thing. He and a lady friend of his, Frankie, whom I also knew, came and picked me up and took me to a nice restaurant for dinner. I was very depressed now and not at all hungry. I didn't feel like visiting, but I did not want to be alone either.

At some point during our dinner, I mentioned that I really did not feel like living anymore. Harry took me quite seriously. That evening, while back at home, I received a phone call from Harry. He was checking to see that I was okay. An hour later, Frankie called me. This continued every hour all night long. They were true friends. No one from Household of Faith Church ever called to see how I was doing.

When I got up in the morning, I went out and looked for my children. I followed the school bus that Steve and Tim rode to school. When the bus arrived at Cedar Grove School, neither Steve nor Tim got off. My heart sank. I went inside and talked with the school principal. I was hoping she would have some answers for me. She told me that Candy had telephoned the school and said there had been a death in the family, and they were going to Iowa.

The principal was concerned about me. She said I appeared to be in shock and asked me if I was going to be okay. I don't remember what I told her, but I immediately got up and left. I went to work but wasn't able to do much. I shared my story so everyone knew what I was going through and why I was behaving so strangely.

Two days later when I telephoned one of Candy's relatives in Thurman, Iowa, she told me Candy and the boys were there. I caught the first plane I could and headed for Iowa. My parents picked me up at the airport and took me to their home in Council Bluffs. I then borrowed my mother's car and drove to Thurman, Iowa. Candy was very surprised to see me. I guess she did not believe I would fly out there. She probably didn't even know that I was aware of where they were. I tried for a couple of days to persuade Candy to come back to Maryland, and my in-laws even allowed me to spend the night in one of their extra bedrooms.

The next day, Candy told me she thought I was crazy, and she really meant it! I asked her if she would come back to Maryland if I admitted myself to a psychiatric hospital and stayed until the doctor said I was okay. It was my understanding that her answer was yes. She had one of her brothers telephone the hospital and make arrangements. I don't know what he said to them, but they said I could come over and be admitted right away. Candy and the brother who had made the phone call drove me to the hospital. When I arrived there, they admitted me and then had me sit and write a letter, stating why I thought I needed psychiatric help.

I didn't know it at the time, but they had Candy write a letter also. Candy's letter apparently made me sound very ill and dangerous. I think she was trying to see that I be kept there for a very long time. Two weeks passed, and Candy never came to see me or even bothered to telephone me.

During my two-week stay at the hospital, I was given a number of written tests, and I attended a few group therapy sessions. At the end of two weeks, I was having a conversation with the psychiatrist. While we were talking, he tried to provoke me to anger. I believed some of what he was saying was way out of line, and he was successful in provoking me. He then asked me, "Did you realize you were angry?"

I said I did, and he told me he thought I handled myself very well. He then told me that for the past two weeks, they had tried to provoke me and see the kind of behavior Candy had described but had not. He told me the various tests they had given me had all shown me to be normal, whatever that is.

The aptitude test I took at that time showed me to be slightly above average. He said I was released but suggested I go back to my job in Maryland and not be concerned about Candy. I did make another attempt at persuading Candy to return, but she would not. Flying back to Maryland alone was one of the most difficult things I had ever done. I had no idea when I would see my family again.

I had not been back in Maryland long when I was served with divorce papers. Candy had filed for divorce even before she left Maryland. She had apparently been planning this for quite a while.

I went back to work, but going home to the empty house every night was difficult. I did not like being alone. The idea came to me that I should run an ad in the newspaper and advertise to rent one of the extra bedrooms. It was very comforting to have someone move into the house with me. This guy was a complete stranger, but the first night he was there, I slept better than I had for a long time. I eventually rented out the second room and had two men living in the house with me. Both of them were Christians, and we got along fine. I continued to pray that God would heal my marriage. I wrote Candy many long love letters. I would sometimes write several times a week. There was never any response from Candy, and I was not able to talk with either of my sons. I was very depressed and decided I could use some professional counseling. I began seeing Dave Williams at Mt. Airy Full Gospel Church. I had been seeing him once a week for a couple of months. It was now December and getting close to Christmas. In one of my letters, I told Candy that I was going to come out and see her and our sons at Christmastime. When I was driving to see Dave Williams the week before I was to leave for Iowa, I was crying profusely.

Christmas alone was very depressing. I cried even while I was with Mr. Williams. He told me he thought the letters I had been writing to Candy had to have had some positive impact on her. He said he had a feeling my trip to Iowa would be fruitful, and perhaps Candy and I could reconcile.

I was really encouraged now and looking forward to the trip. I purchased Christmas presents for Candy, Steve, and Tim and took them with me on the plane. I rented a car when I arrived in Omaha and first drove to my parents' house in Council Bluffs. I visited with my parents for a while, but I was really excited about seeing my family again, so I headed for Thurman, Iowa. I arrived, only to find that they were not there. They had gone into hiding someplace, and no one would tell me where. I left the presents for them and drove back to my parents' house, crying the entire way.

I loved my parents, but I was very depressed and did not want to be there. I called the airlines, and they let me take an early flight back to Maryland. I am sure that was the worst Christmas I had ever experienced. I was really glad when December was over.

Just before it was time for the scheduled court hearing, Pastor Roger Melson called a special meeting at his house. There were six people there, including me. Roger had learned of the upcoming court hearing, and some of the members of Household of Faith Church were going to testify in court. He was concerned that there might be some friction among certain church members, so he wanted to have this private meeting to "clear the air," so to speak, before the actual court hearing.

It turned out to be a most interesting meeting. I learned that two of the people present at the meeting had actually helped Candy move out. I was really shocked! Two other people there were going to testify in my behalf. These two people in the church had actually helped my wife and children leave me and pretended for an entire year that they knew nothing. When I had first learned that my family was gone, I was frantic. I had no idea where they were. These people, including the pastor, knew and said nothing to me. I could hardly believe that my brothers and sisters in the Lord could have done such a thing. There was never an apology, but I knew I had to forgive them anyway.

I continued to write love letters to Candy, Steve, and Tim. There was never any response. I knew they were receiving my letters because I would send checks to Candy, and she would always sign and cash them. I was certain that God would eventually heal my marriage. I even promised my sons that we would all be together again. I continued to be counseled by Mr. Williams, until he suggested that it was not necessary that I see him anymore.

Many months passed, and I still didn't hear from Candy or my sons. Some people suggested to me that I hire an attorney. I did not want to do that. It seemed to me to be the wrong thing to do. However, after several more months with no communication, I decided I had to make a move. I hired a Christian attorney. I offered Candy $10,000 to buy her out so I would own the house. She refused my offer. I was forced to sell the house. When all was said and done, we each ended up with $10,000, but neither of us had a house.

Here in Maryland, $10,000 isn't much toward buying a house. I wanted to stay in Damascus, and I did finally find a town house I was able to afford. Candy was ordered to return to Maryland for a child-custody hearing. She and one of her cousins made the trip. Candy's mother came also to testify in court in Candy's behalf.

Candy's attorney tried to provoke me to anger while I was on the stand in the courtroom. He was not able to do so. He, in fact, became angry at his failure, turned red-faced, and stomped his foot on the floor. He tried to prove to the court that I was an unfit parent because of my strong religious beliefs. When I wrote a letter in the mail, I would write, "Jesus is Lord" on the bottom corner of the envelope. Candy's attorney tried to make it sound like I was some kind of unstable fanatic. For whatever reason, Candy was awarded full custody of our sons. I was given visitation rights and ordered to pay child support and health insurance for my sons.

A New Chapter

This chapter was a verbatim letter written to Master James L. Ryan of the circuit court for Montgomery County, Maryland. In the letter, I chastised Mr. Ryan for making, what I believed, was a wrong decision in awarding Candy full custody of our sons. The letter was nine pages in length and gave me much room to criticize and make degrading remarks about Candy.

Upon reading the first printing of this book, one of the pastors at Covenant Life Church suggested that if I were to ever do a reprint of the book, I would do well to eliminate this chapter. Well, the time for a reprint did come, but I decided to try a rewrite rather than eliminate the entire chapter.

It has been four years since the original writing. My family and I have continued attending Covenant Life Church. I believe that during the past four years, I have continued to grow in the ways of our Lord. For one thing, it is much easier now for me to see how negative the letter to Mr. Ryan was. I'm sure that four years ago, I would not have accepted the pastor's advice but would have become defensive and self-righteous.

I had convinced myself that including the letter would allow my two adult sons to read it and know that I really loved them and made every possible effort to be granted custody of them when they were young boys. However, it is more likely that I included the letter to give myself an opportunity to point out to my sons some of the sins of their mother. Candy was not without sin, but this book is about me and how God worked to bring about change in my life. Therefore, there is no need to mention anything that, in my opinion, Candy was guilty of. Although I can appreciate your curiosity concerning Candy's behavior, I will remain silent. I feel that it is the man's responsibility to keep his marriage together. In short, I failed. When I had learned that Candy and our sons had returned to Iowa, I made plane reservations and flew out there as soon as I possibly could. I did my best to persuade Candy to return to Maryland with me. However, because of my past sinful behavior, she was still terrified of me and refused to return.

I wept as I left Iowa, not knowing when I'd ever see my sons again. I was depressed and didn't feel like returning to work or doing anything else for that matter. God did sustain me through this very difficult time. I decided I would benefit from more counseling and once again began seeing Dave Williams at Mt. Airy Full Gospel Church. I met with Mr. Williams on a regular basis for nearly six months until Mr. Williams suggested to me that he thought I had learned what I had set out to learn. He then saw no need for me to have any further visits with him unless I felt the need to do so.

What I set out to learn was primarily to trust God more fully while going through difficult times. All the counseling I received from Mr. Williams was based on biblical scripture.

During Jesus's thirty-some years here on earth, He never said a bad word nor had a negative thought about anyone. He expressed love for even those who did Him wrong. He was ridiculed, scorned, and finally tortured and crucified. Even with all this done to Him, He continued to love those who hurt Him, and He forgave them. So I said to myself, "Here I am, a sinner. I am not perfect. I didn't love my wife with agape love. I did, to some degree, mistreat my wife. I was certainly more concerned about my own well-being than hers, so what right do I have to feel sorry for myself?"

The answer, of course, is none. I am simply reaping what I have sown. All sin has its consequences, and we must live with those consequences no matter what they might be. We are truly blessed to have a loving, merciful God who is quick to forgive us when we repent of our sins. He doesn't take away the consequences, but He helps us deal with them, and He shows us how to be at peace.

I once read that the best thing a man can do for his children is to love their mother. Whether or not it is the best thing, I cannot say, but it certainly is a good thing. I only wish that I had done so before my marriage ended in divorce. I am only now learning how to love with unconditional agape love. It's not easy, but I shall work at it as long as I live.

The court granted me certain visitation rights with my sons. The geographical distance between my sons and me is about 1,200 miles. I had only ten days of paid vacation, so to drive to Iowa and then drive back to Maryland with my sons was completely out of the question. Six of my ten vacation days would have been spent just driving. I believed there was no way I could support myself, send child support money to Iowa, and be able to save enough money to buy round-trip plane tickets for my sons. At the time, the situation seemed hopeless to me. I believed I would be spending very little, if any, time with my sons.

However, all was not lost. God, once again, in His mercy and goodness, provided a way. I believe He always will if we will just stop worrying and place our trust in Him. When summer arrived and it was time for visitation, my mother, who also lived in Iowa, agreed to help me with airfare. Not only did she help me financially, but she agreed to fly to Maryland with my sons and stay an entire month so I could have more time with my sons. Every summer thereafter, it always worked out that my sons could make the trip. Sometimes they came for only two weeks, but we made certain our time was well spent.

Then Comes Glenna

Candy would send me a copy of Steve's and Tim's report cards from school. Otherwise, I would not hear from her. I did continue to write letters, and I continued to pray for the healing of my marriage. Even though I had rented out part of my house and there were two men living with me, I was lonely. It was some time before I came to the conclusion that Candy had no plan of ever reconciling with me. About two years had passed, but I had not yet given up hope.

Harry Down, a friend and neighbor, knew I was a Christian. His ex-wife knew a single lady who was also Christian. Harry and his ex-wife decided that because this lady and I were both single and Christian, we would be a perfect match for each other. I thought the idea was pretty silly, but I accepted her telephone number from Harry, and after a couple of days, I decided to give her a call. This was my first but not last conversation with Glenna Sue Shazer. Glenna was packing to go to Ocean City, Maryland, for a week. We visited for a while, and I told her I would call her in a week or so when she returned.

I did call Glenna again. Her week at Ocean City probably passed quickly. For me, it went slowly. I was anxious about calling Glenna again and had been counting down the days. During our second conversation, I learned that Glenna had been married twice before and had a six-year-old son. Her first marriage was very short. Her husband was into drugs and was abusive to her. Unfortunately, her next husband, the father of her son, was pretty much the same. Louie was abusive to Glenna and to Brian as well. Glenna finally left him for the safety of herself and Brian.

Sometime after Glenna had left Louie Shazer, she became a Christian. One of her longtime female friends had led her to the Lord. Glenna and I decided that we would like to meet each other. I believe it was on a Sunday afternoon. I do remember that it was August 10, 1986. It was Brian's birthday. He had just turned seven years of age.

Glenna and I met at a park in Gaithersburg. It was a beautiful day, and there were a lot of people in the park. I arrived first and awaited Glenna's arrival. It was my intention from the start that the relationship between Glenna and me would be platonic. Nevertheless, I was curious and somewhat concerned about her appearance. Harry had already told me that Glenna was a cute little thing. When a car with a single lady driver pulled into the parking lot, I knew it was Glenna. I don't usually remember what a person was wearing the previous day, but I can still remember what Glenna was wearing then. I think what stood out the most was her deep, dark tan. And Harry was right. She was a cute little thing.

I remember how she waved to me. I don't think I have ever seen her wave like that to anyone since. Glenna and I walked around the lake and talked with each other very easily. I was honest with Glenna right from the start. I told her I was still legally married and had two sons. I told her also that I was still praying for my marriage to be healed. Glenna and I took a liking to each other, and I continued to talk with her on the phone often. We had not known each other very long when I asked Glenna if she would like to go on a one-day cruise with me from Annapolis, Maryland, to the Inner Harbor in Baltimore, Maryland. She agreed, and it turned out to be a wonderful day.

We did not do a very good job at keeping the relationship platonic, though. It wasn't long before we were holding hands, and I had my arm around her while we were on the boat. I did feel guilty, but I enjoyed being with Glenna. We had a lot of fun together. We talked on the phone almost every evening and would spend most of our Saturdays and Sundays together. We did not spend the night together. I would go home on Saturday evening and then see Glenna on Sunday morning.

Glenna was attending a Baptist church, and I attended Household of Faith Church. Glenna went to Household of Faith church with me once. A few of the ladies there knew I was praying for my marriage to Candy to be healed, and they were too. Glenna felt very uncomfortable at Household of Faith and went just the one time. Sometimes when Glenna and I were together, we would hold hands and pray for the healing of my marriage. The holding-of-hands part was not a good idea!

Glenna had told me that since she became a Christian, she had not been dating. She had prayed that God would bring the man to be her husband to her front door. Glenna believed that man was me. I told her I thought it could not be since I was still legally married and was praying for my marriage to be healed. She agreed that was probably true.

Brian was a well-behaved, well-mannered boy. He didn't seem to mind that I had entered his mother's life. The three of us spent a lot of time together. It was sometimes difficult for me, though. I never have been much of a sportsman, but I took Brian fishing one day. I wanted to talk with him and see how he really felt about his mother and me spending so much time together. His dad did not spend time or communicate with Brian, and Brian did not at all mind me becoming a part of his and his mother's lives, at least not at first.

When Mike was very ill, Candy and I bought a special chair just for Mike. It was an overstuffed recliner. Mike needed the comfortable chair, and he was the only one who used it. When Candy left Maryland, the chair was one of the few things she left behind. She did finally take it with her, though, when she came back for one of the court hearings. In the meantime, while I still had the chair, Glenna and Brian came over to my house to visit. Brian sat down in the recliner, and I struggled at seeing him there. No one else had sat in that chair, and it didn't seem right to me that Brian was sitting there. Of course, neither Brian nor Glenna had any idea that the chair had been Mike's. I finally convinced myself that it was just a chair, and it didn't matter.

I didn't spend a great deal of time with Brian, but when I did, I felt guilty. I couldn't really be a father figure to my sons in Iowa anymore, and it somehow didn't seem right that I would be a father figure to Brian.

Glenna and I had been dating for about a year when Pastor Melson had invited a well-known Christian prophet to visit our church. By now, Glenna and I had become very serious about each other and were wondering what to do. We prayed to God and asked Him to give us an answer through Mike Ratliff, the prophet, whether or not we should get married. Neither Glenna nor I had ever met this man until the night of the service. A half hour or so into the service, Mr. Ratliff approached Glenna and me. He said, "You aren't married, are you?"

We told him we were not, and he asked us to stand. He then gave us a few words of prophecy. Glenna and I did not receive a specific answer concerning marriage, but because we were told that we would be praying together for people, we took it as a yes.

The ladies at the Household of Faith who were praying for Candy and me to be together again were at the prophecy service and heard the prophecy that was given to Glenna and me. They were pretty upset with me a couple of days later when I told them I was no longer praying for my marriage to Candy to be healed. They believed we had misinterpreted the prophecy. They believed Glenna and I could have a ministry together without being married to each other. From that time on, there was a lot of tension between the ladies and Glenna and me.

Sometime later, the man who helped Candy leave me and then kept it a secret for a year was being considered as an elder in the church. I remember Pastor Melson asking if there was opposition to this man becoming an elder in light of some previous event that he had been involved in. As I recall, no one in the congregation voiced an opinion at that time. I did learn later that there was some opposition. I believe Pastor Melson allowed compromise to take place in the church, and now there was division.

I decided it would be best if I left Household of Faith Church. Glenna and I started attending a very similar church meeting at Cedar Grove Elementary School in Damascus. This church was called Damascus Covenant Church, and the pastor was Bill Woodrow. In addition to being pastor, Bill Woodrow owned a company called Dye Team. Quite a few of the men in the church were employed by Dye Team. I thought it was something that I'd never want to do.

It wasn't long after I left Household of Faith Church that I heard that the number of people there was beginning to dwindle. The Household of Faith Church finally ceased to exist. I was not surprised. The Bible says, "A house divided against itself cannot stand." There was division in the Household of Faith Church, and that church fell.

I believe Pastor Roger Melson did then and still does love our Lord very much. I believe he was in error in some of his decision-making regarding the church. I also believe he has learned and repented. I love Roger Melson and hold no grudge against him or any former members of Household of Faith Church.

Glenna and I joined a care group at Damascus Covenant Church and were recognized as a couple. However, we—mostly I—were still not completely certain what God's will was for us. Over the course of several years, we caused each other much pain. We would decide to get married, and then I would have doubts and call it off. On one occasion, we did become engaged, but I would never set a specific date for the wedding, so Glenna got discouraged and called it off.

I was really depressed during this time. Our church care group leader knew of our history together and saw how depressed I was and said to me, "Why don't you and Glenna just get married?" I guess that was the final little push I needed. Once again, I asked Glenna to marry me. She made me wait for a couple of days before she said yes. I had learned from my sons in Iowa that their mother had remarried in January of 1989. Hearing that news caused me to believe I was completely released from any further obligation to my relationship with Candy. Dennis Cook Jr., our care group leader, was also an ordained minister, so on June 30, 1989, he officiated as Glenna and I became husband and wife.

We had a small wedding that was held at the Colony Clubhouse in Germantown, Maryland. My two sons came out from Iowa, and they and Brian all took part in the wedding ceremony. Glenna and I spent our first night together in my town house. The next morning Glenna, Steve, Tim, Brian, and my nephew Jerry Richardson all left for Ocean City, Maryland. This was to be our honeymoon. It felt great being married to Glenna, and I was sure the right decision had been made. With our entourage, we had a great time on our one-week honeymoon.

In the three years that Glenna and I dated each other before we got married, we had many conversations concerning many topics. We thought we knew each other pretty well. However, we eventually learned that we assumed a lot about each other. By the grace of God, we were able to work out the majority of our disagreements and misunderstandings. In fact, we are still working them out.

There is one very important thing we should have done before we became married to each other. It would have eliminated a number of surprises and made our lives together easier. We should have gone through premarital counseling. In my opinion, no couple should become married without first going through premarital counseling. That is where all the tough questions are answered, like who is going to be responsible for paying what, if any, bill? Will we have joint or separate checking accounts? What about children? Will we have any? If so, how will we discipline them? If my wife and I both have an income, is her income hers or ours? I may believe in tithing 10 percent of our income to the church; my wife may not. Glenna and I struggled through many issues that should have been discussed and agreed upon before we became married. It is my belief also that no pastor should perform a wedding ceremony for a couple that was previously married unless each of them can state how he or she contributed to the failure of the first marriage.

When Glenna and I first shared the news of our marriage plans with Brian, he was happy. He was now going to have a dad. Brian and I probably should have received some counseling too because we had some differing views about a father-son relationship. I really never did know what Brian expected, but I think he had the idea that as his dad I would be more of a playmate, someone to take him fishing, to ball games, and perhaps play ball with him. I, on the other hand, saw myself as being a role model to teach him how to become a good Christian man. I was to teach him good work habits and discipline, for example.

Once Glenna and I were married, many unexpected changes were introduced into Brian's life. I believed it would be better for Brian if we took him out of the public school system and put him in a Christian school. We enrolled him in Ets Chaiyim, which was a Messianic Jewish school. They had Brian tested and said they would accept him as a student, but because they were so advanced compared to the public school, Brian would have to be put back not one but two grade levels! This and other changes made life more difficult for Brian. I think he began to see me more as an intruder into his and his mother's lives than as a blessing. I was not good at expressing love toward Brian, and when I did tell him I loved him, he didn't seem to believe me.

Glenna continued working her job with the federal government, and I continued working for Southern Optical. We did have an occasional dispute but never anything serious. I think many of our disagreements concerned Glenna's son Brian in one way or another. I believe it was the summer of 1987 when I began to feel ill.

My sons Steve and Tim had come from Iowa to spend two weeks with me, and I had taken off work so we could spend time together. I wanted to make good use of the time we had together, but I really had to force myself to get up and do anything. I felt somewhat like I had the flu. My stomach felt nauseated, and I was greatly lacking in energy. Once I would force myself to be active, I would usually feel a little better. Unfortunately, the condition never went away. I went to see the doctor, and several tests were done, but there was never a conclusive answer.

A Korean woman who worked at the contact lens lab was familiar with acupuncture. She was sure it was just what I needed. Thinking I had nothing to lose, I gave it a try. It was actually relaxing, and it worked. Unfortunately, my insurance company wouldn't cover the cost, and the nausea returned when the acupuncture was discontinued. After enduring the condition for a while, I decided there had to be an answer, so I switched doctors and started the testing over again. I was somewhat concerned that I may have somehow contracted the AIDS virus, but I decided to let the doctor finish all the testing he thought necessary and see what the end result was. If he didn't come up with an answer I could accept, I was going to ask him to give me a test for AIDS.

None of the tests I was given came back positive, but the doctor was pretty sure my condition was due to a chemical imbalance in the brain. He said it was causing me to have a physical depression, and he wanted me to start taking Prozac. I really didn't understand. I had heard some stories about Prozac, and I wasn't sure I wanted to start taking an antidepressant. At least the expense was going to be covered by my insurance company, so although I didn't really believe it would work, I started taking Prozac daily. It was gradual, but after about two weeks, I did notice an improvement. I took Prozac every day throughout the winter months.

When summer arrived I discontinued so I would see what would happen. I felt fine and assumed I no longer had this problem. However, once fall arrived, I began to feel nauseated again and had to go back on the Prozac. The doctor was not surprised. He said many people suffer from this same condition, and it did seem to be seasonal. He concluded that a lack of sunlight during the winter months was a contributor to the cause. I have been taking Prozac on and off for about twelve years now.

Argument with Glenna

One evening in 1995, Glenna and I had a pretty serious argument. I can't even recall what it was about. I would guess it had something to do with Brian, her son. In her anger, Glenna told me she was going to divorce me. I really didn't know if she was serious, but I assumed she was. I was not about to go through a second divorce, so I foolishly and compulsively went upstairs and took a bottle of muscle relaxers plus a few painkillers. I told Glenna what I had done, and then I left the house. I took off in the five-speed Mazda 626 we owned at that time.

The effect of the pills began to work very quickly. I first drove to the Damascus Shopping Center. From there, I made a phone call to Glenna, and I think I asked her to tell my sons that I loved them. I then drove to Germantown, Maryland, which was only about fifteen minutes away. I pulled into a gas station and made another call to Glenna. I really don't remember much of what was said. I know I asked her once again to tell my sons that I loved them.

As groggy as I was, my thinking was still clear enough that I knew I had to get off the phone before the call could be traced. Glenna had informed me that she had telephoned Bill Woodrow, my pastor and now employer, and the police and that people were looking for me.

I got back into the car and began to drive. I remember that I was crying. I could barely tell what I was doing, and I surely don't know how I was able to shift gears in the car. I really believed my life was about to be over.

As I drove and cried, I prayed that God would forgive me, and I asked Him that no one would be injured as a result of my reckless driving. Eventually, I blacked out. I remember paramedics being gathered around the car door and asking one of the paramedics how they happened to arrive there so quickly. She said they were returning en route from another call.

Of course, I had no idea how long I had been there. I had no idea how far I had made it from the gas station or where I was. I think I had driven up onto a median and run into a road sign. I remember a male paramedic lightly slapping my face and saying, "Stay with us now," but I didn't. I had blacked out again.

When I awoke, I was riding in an ambulance. This time, there was no hurry. I was simply being transferred to another hospital. I learned the rest from Glenna. She said the police had telephoned her and told her that they had found me and that I was being rushed to Shady Grove Hospital. Mike Vario, a pastor from Damascus Covenant Church, went to the hospital when he learned I was there. Glenna said he wasn't allowed in the emergency room, but he was in the hall just outside it, pacing the floor and praying for me.

Glenna said I gave the doctors in the emergency room a very rough time. Apparently, I was tossing and fighting with them, causing them to have a difficult time getting me strapped to the table. I have no memory of this.

I think it was about three in the morning when I woke up in an ambulance and discovered that I was being transferred to Washington Adventist Hospital in Takoma Park, Maryland. Upon arrival at the hospital, I discovered that I was being taken to the psychiatric ward. I had experienced that before, and I was not happy.

While I was lying on a gurney in the hall, waiting for a room to become ready, I asked the nurse if I could use the men's room. After relieving myself, I began to vomit profusely. Apparently, doctors at Shady Grove Hospital had pumped some sort of liquid charcoal into my stomach. I later learned that this was routine practice. The purpose of the charcoal was to absorb from my stomach any of the harmful medications I had ingested. The vomiting I experienced was not routine, but hey, a man has to do what a man has to do.

The next thing I remembered is that it was morning, and Bill Woodrow and another friend were standing over my bed. Bill told me how he had been out looking for me the previous evening and how much worry I had caused so many people. He said he was thankful that I was okay. I didn't tell him how embarrassed I was.

My stay in the hospital lasted one week. The doctors there decided I was in good health, both physically and mentally. They attributed my episode of attempted suicide to my having been off Prozac. They told me to be sure to stay on my medication, then they released me. I believe my not being on Prozac had nothing whatsoever to do with the episode, but I didn't argue with them. I just left as quickly as I was able to.

So why did I do it? Did I really want to die? No! Was it a cry for help? I don't think so. It was a very stupid, compulsive act that I'm sure I will never commit again. But I did, and I thank God that I am still alive.

As I previously stated, I didn't remember what the argument was about that caused Glenna to say she wanted a divorce, which caused me to take a bunch of pills. So before writing this next section, I decided it would be wise to talk to Glenna and see what information she could offer. I didn't want to open old wounds in doing so, but I asked Glenna if she recalled what the argument on that particular evening was about. No wounds were opened because Glenna had no memory of what we argued about either.

Glenna did mention something that I still do not recall, but I'm not sure her recollection is correct. According to Glenna, there were various times when she and I would have an argument or disagreement, and I would threaten her with a divorce. She said she knew I didn't mean it, but I had made that statement again on the particular evening, and that was the final straw for her. So she said she would give me a divorce, and she meant it!

She apparently began making plans right away. About two months after I had been released from the hospital, Glenna informed me that she had found a place to rent and that she and Brian were moving out. I was devastated, of course, and tried to persuade Glenna to do otherwise. She didn't, though, and she told me she would be gone for at least a year. This was because she had signed a year's lease on a town house. Glenna moved out on a Sunday.

I was extremely depressed! I went to Damascus Covenant Church, which at this time had been renamed Word of Life Church and made a move to Frederick, Maryland. The church was previously in Damascus, Maryland.

I was a sad case to say the least! I cried the entire drive from Damascus to Frederick. My shoelaces were untied, and upon arriving, I walked into the church crying and sat off to the side by myself. After the service, Pastor Mike Vario mentioned that there was a brother in the church who was really hurting and suggested that some might pray with me. Many did, and I was moved! People I didn't even know came to pray for me. I was still very depressed but had at least stopped crying.

On the way out of the building, a friend of mine, Dennis Cook Sr., said he was glad to see that I had at least tied my shoes. I phoned my sister Linda, and knowing how distraught I was, she drove down from Waldorf, Maryland, to spend the day with me. Linda and I sat and visited while Glenna went about her business with the final packing.

The first week was the most difficult. I had to force myself to go to work. As it turned out, Glenna had rented a town house in the same development and was just down the street from me. I guess she didn't see any need to put a great deal of distance between the two of us. She was on her own now and making her own decisions.

At Brian's request, Glenna took him out of the Christian school and enrolled him in Damascus High School, a public school. In my opinion, that was not a good idea because Brian was weak when it came to peer pressure, and he was easily pulled down by others.

Glenna never filed for a divorce. In fact, we visited on the phone often and went out together almost every Friday evening. I soon decided to rent out a bedroom and advertised for a guy to move in with me. Having this guy live with me was better than being in an empty house, but I wanted my wife to be living with me.

After six months or so, I was extremely frustrated with the situation. I wasn't depressed anymore, but I felt like I was living in limbo. I didn't like it at all. It seemed to me that Glenna wanted to have her cake and eat it too, and I had come to the conclusion that Glenna was not going to come back. I wanted to get on with my life with some definite answers. At one point, I talked on the phone with an attorney about filing for a legal separation.

I left the Word of Life Church in Frederick. I had heard about Covenant Life Church in Gaithersburg and decided to check it out. I knew this church had a very large congregation, and I thought it would be easier for me to find a new Christian wife.

I felt uncomfortable during my first visit because of the size of the congregation. Finally, I saw someone I knew from a previous church I had attended and sat with him. After the service, he introduced me to one of the many pastors, Kenneth Maresco. I told him that my wife had deserted me, and I believed that I had grounds for divorce. Kenneth told me that he didn't think I had grounds for divorce, but he would be glad to counsel me if I was interested. I was, so I telephoned the church office and made an appointment with him.

When the day of my appointment with the attorney arrived, I went and saw her. I informed her that I wanted to put things on hold and that I was going to continue to pray for my marriage to be healed.

Pregnancy Announced

I went to see Kenneth Maresco at Covenant Life Church. Kenneth was kind but very serious. He said he was glad to be able to offer counseling to me but that I would have to show my sincerity and do the work assignments he gave me. He wanted to hear nothing at all about Glenna but focused only on me and how I could change. It was tough work. I wasn't even sure I could do what he was asking of me. I just took it a day at a time, though, and did the best I could.

While I was being counseled by Kenneth, I was also attending classes to become a member of the church. I still struggled a lot and wasn't certain about my future. I started attending a care group at Covenant Life Church, but I was no longer wearing my wedding ring.

Most of my Christian friends saw no hope for my marriage and, therefore, encouraged me to move on. There were only two couples who were insistent that I continue to pray for my marriage to be healed. Dennis and Barbara Cook and Kathy and Jonathan Holmes would not listen to any of my talk about looking for a new wife. When visiting with Dennis Cook, I would sometimes try to justify my less-than-biblical thinking. I would say something to Dennis like, "According to the Bible, I think I can do/think whatever," but Dennis, at the risk of jeopardizing our friendship, would say, "Well, that's not what I think!"

Kathy and Jonathan Holmes would occasionally invite Glenna and me over to their house. I would usually go by myself, but they did not stop treating us as a couple. They would usually remind me of some particular scripture that I needed to hear. I continued what I believed to be very difficult counseling sessions with Kenneth Maresco, and I slowly began to grow more in the ways of our Lord.

Perhaps Glenna saw some change in me or maybe just because of the power of prayer and conviction, she visited Covenant Life Church with me and began to see Kenneth Maresco also.

I finally telephoned someone from the care group I was attending at the church and apologized to her for not wearing my wedding ring and for giving her a false impression. I decided to begin wearing my wedding ring again although Glenna was not yet wearing hers.

The end of Glenna's lease was drawing near, and she needed to make a decision. She prayed that God would do a few things to make it clear to her what she was to do. I know Glenna had made several requests of God, but neither she nor I can remember what they were, except for one. The owner of the town house Glenna was living in had decided to sell the place. There was another town house right across the street, which was also for sale. Glenna asked God to cause the town house she was living in to sell quickly if he wanted her to move back in with me. The town house across the street was somewhat nicer than the one Glenna was living in, and they were asking less money for it than the one Glenna was in. However, the first people who looked at the house Glenna was living in made the decision to buy it.

Although there had been a couple of other requests made to God by Glenna, that answered prayer was all she needed to make her decision. She was going to move back in with me! It was July, and Glenna would have to move out by the end of August.

A few nights later, Glenna invited me to go shopping with her. While we were strolling through the mall, Glenna stopped at a jewelry store and picked up a ring she had left there to be sized. Even though she immediately put it on her finger, it wasn't until sometime later, before leaving the mall, that I realized that it was her wedding ring.

Glenna was still living in her rented town house with about a month remaining. She was slowly getting her and Brian's belongings packed. One evening, she telephoned me and asked me to come over right away. I couldn't imagine what it was all about. She sounded very excited.

As soon as I arrived, she said, "You're not going to believe this!"

I said, "What, what?"

Well she was right, I really couldn't believe it! She said, "I'm pregnant!"

I immediately left for the drugstore and bought another pregnancy test. The result of the second test was the same. Glenna was pregnant! At that time, I was forty-seven years of age, and Glenna was forty-one.

Although my firstborn son had died, I had two surviving sons, and Glenna had Brian. We had decided from the beginning of our relationship that we would not have children together. God obviously had other plans for us. Glenna became pregnant even though we were using birth control at the time. This was in God's timing, though! He waited until we were ready. Our reason for not wanting children was nothing less than selfishness. We didn't want the expense or responsibility. But now, we were excited!

We were both thinking that we were too old to be having a baby, but since it was God's will for us, we would just thank Him and be the best parents we could be. I told the guy renting the room from me that he would have to find another place. Glenna and Brian soon moved back in.

Brian wasn't happy, though. He had a lot more freedom while he was living down the street than he would have now. He had gotten in with the wrong crowd and was getting into some trouble. He had dropped out of school but later got his general education diploma. I'm not quite sure what Brian thought about his mother being pregnant.

The nine months passed quickly, at least for me. Glenna and I had taken birthing classes at Holy Cross Hospital, but her doctor decided it would be best if she delivered by cesarean. We knew ahead of time that we were going to have a son. Glenna wanted to name him Sean Michael. I had no problem with that at all. Although Glenna had heard it, she did not remember that my son Timothy's middle name is Sean, and Michael was the first name of my son who died.

On the day Sean was born, March 24, 1997, I was in the delivery room with Glenna. After Sean was delivered and checked out, the doctor brought him to me to hold. As he was handing Sean to me, he said, "We won't know for certain until a blood test is done, but there are several indications that he may have Down syndrome."

The doctor pointed out some of the signs, which included the shape of his eyes and the creases in the palms of his hands, which ran straight across rather than diagonally. Sean also had an additional little thumb on his right hand. The doctor said that was not uncommon for Down syndrome babies but that it could be surgically removed when Sean was older, which it was.

Other than being surprised to hear this news about Down syndrome, I didn't really know how to respond. For Glenna's benefit, I acted as though everything was fine and normal. I learned later that Glenna had believed that all along. The fact that Sean might have Down syndrome didn't affect her at all. I loved Sean before he was born, and the fact that he had Down syndrome didn't change that at all. He was still my son, and I loved him.

However, as I was driving home from the hospital that evening, I broke into tears. I wasn't even sure why I was crying, but I remember saying to myself as I wept, "My son has Down syndrome." I didn't even know for sure what Down syndrome was or how our lives would be affected. I think I was just having a pity party for myself because my son wasn't perfect. I accepted the fact very quickly, though, and thanked God for giving Glenna and me such a precious little child.

The blood test did confirm that Sean had Down syndrome, and as a result of a hearing test that they had given him, they told us they thought he was deaf. That was a little difficult for me to deal with, but I finally told myself that Glenna and I would just have to learn sign language.

We were soon able to take Sean home with us, and we received much support. Montgomery County offered many programs to parents of children with disabilities. Various therapists from the infants and toddlers program began to come to our house to give Sean speech and physical therapy. We soon learned of an organization called Parents of Down's Syndrome (PODS). We met many other parents with Down syndrome children and received much information and support.

Our little dog Shadow was anything but quiet. One day while Sean was on the floor sleeping, Shadow heard a noise outside and responded with his usual loud bark. We noticed Sean jump! We continued to watch as these occurrences took place and were soon convinced that Sean wasn't totally deaf. Later on, when another hearing test was administered, it was learned that Sean's hearing was fine. Apparently, there had been fluid in his ears when the first test was given, and the result was not accurate.

On the evening of February 22, 1998, we had Sean lying on a blanket on the living room floor. I was there beside him. All of a sudden, Glenna and I heard what sounded like a gunshot. At about that same moment, a shotgun round came through the carpet just next to Sean and me. I ran downstairs to find Brian lying on his back in a pool of blood. He had bent over and shot himself in the stomach with a twelve-gauge shotgun. The round had passed through Brian's body, gone through the basement ceiling, and finally lodged in the ceiling above where Sean and I had been lying.

Brian was still alive, but judging from the amount of blood loss, I suspected he would not live long. I said to him, "Why, Brian?"

He slightly moved his head but said nothing. I was sure his life was about over. I told him that I loved him and then said to him, "Go and be with Jesus."

Glenna had already telephoned the paramedics in Damascus. It seemed it was taking them a very long time to get there. I ran upstairs and saw the ambulance stopped at the end of the street. I couldn't imagine what they were doing, so I ran out into the street and motioned for them to come down to the house. The ambulance moved very slowly. It was finally in front of the house, but no one was getting out. I was frantic! I started shouting at them. "Come on," I said. "My son is lying on the floor dying!"

They said they were not allowed to go into the house until a police officer arrived and made sure it was all clear.

Glenna was on the phone with the 911 people, telling them what was happening. They told Glenna to go and move the gun and tell the paramedics when it was safe to go in. At about the same time, a police officer arrived and gave the all clear signal to the paramedics. They immediately began to administer medical treatment to Brian, but there was little they could do. They put Brian in the ambulance and drove him to the Damascus High School parking lot, where he was flown by helicopter to Suburban Hospital in Bethesda, Maryland.

Surgeons were waiting for Brian's arrival and began to work immediately. Our care group leader and a couple of pastors from Covenant Life Church sat at the hospital with Glenna and me almost all night long. It was probably about 5:00 a.m. when the surgeon came to us and told us that they were finished. They thought Brian would be all right, but he would need many months of hospitalization and physical therapy. Brian was still asleep, but they let us go and see him. We then went home to get some rest.

We were probably home for no more than two hours when the hospital telephoned us and said we should come back right away. When we arrived back at the hospital, Brian was no longer alive. The doctors hadn't been able to stop the internal bleeding.

Brian had left several suicide notes to several people. In one of them, he said to be sure and tell Sean that he loved him. After the funeral, Brian's natural dad came up to me and said, "Thank you for raising my son."

I said, "I tried, Louie."

Louie then told me, "It wasn't your fault."

I don't know whose fault it was. Perhaps many of us had failed Brian, but ultimately, it was his decision to end his life. We will always miss him!

Since Glenna and I now had Sean, we considered having another child. We both thought it would be nice to have a daughter and that it would be good for Sean also. We didn't use birth control and just left the situation up to God. One year later, God did bless us with a beautiful daughter. On February 24, 1999, she was delivered by cesarean section. We named her Megan Alise. She and Sean have grown to love each other and are wonderful playmates! They probably get along like most siblings. Sometimes they fight with each other, and other times they defend one another. Glenna and I were truly blessed to have these two precious children. When we learned of Glenna's pregnancy with Sean, we thought we were too old to be having a baby. Now here we are with two toddlers. I'm sure they will help keep us young!

In January of 2000, Glenna was diagnosed with breast cancer. In February, a lumpectomy was performed, and chemotherapy was begun. Glenna went through three months of chemotherapy and six weeks of radiation treatments. She underwent the entire experience like a real trooper. She continued to work at her government job the entire time as well as take care of Sean and Megan.

Glenna was to take twenty milligrams of Tamoxifen every day for five years; she has three to go. This drug is supposed to prevent a recurrence of breast cancer, but a possible side effect is that it may cause ovarian cancer. Initially, we had decided that she would not take this drug, but she is taking it at the urging of her doctor. He said the chance of breast cancer recurring is much greater that the chance of her getting ovarian cancer.

A few weeks ago, Glenna was seen by a dermatologist, who removed several moles from her body. The moles were sent to a pathology lab for testing. Glenna received word just last week that one of the moles is dysplastic nevus. This is significant in that someone with dysplastic nevus is considered to have an increased lifetime risk for melanoma. Glenna will have to go back to the dermatologist and have the part of that particular mole that is still under her skin removed. She has several more moles on her body, and she has now been asked to be examined by the dermatologist at least once a year.

Summary of Book 1

So how am I dealing with anger today? Well, first of all, I am no longer controlled by anger, and I don't get angry nearly as often as I used to. I haven't claimed to be a counselor or pastor. I'm just a regular guy who decided to share some of my life's experiences.

Some people, amazed at how I changed, asked me how I did so. There is no formula that I know of, but I will share what worked for me. It was when I was living alone, after my wife and children returned to Iowa, that I recognized a need for serious change. I realized that it was because of my inability to control my anger that I had lost my family and was so miserable. The first step for me was recognizing that I needed to change and decide to do something about it. I sought out a good Christian counselor, and the process began. It has been a long process, and I still work at it today. However, it is much easier than it used to be.

What I have learned most recently has helped me the most. It was through a counselor at Covenant Life Church that I learned a very basic principle: Whenever a person is angry, it is because something is not the way he wants it to be. I have found this to be true in every situation where I begin to feel angry. I ask myself this question: What is it that I want to be different? There is always something! I may feel angry because I believe my wife should behave differently, or maybe the weather caused me to not be able to do something outside that I wanted to do. There is always something I want to be different. When I realize what it is and stop being selfish or assume I know more than God, my anger subsides.

There is, of course, a proper time for anger, so it is not always a sin to be angry. It's how we deal with the anger that makes the difference. When I hear how many babies are killed by abortion every year, it makes me angry. I can do something constructive, like write my representatives in congress or pray. If I let the anger control me and I go and blow up an abortion clinic, I have certainly sinned.

I think most of us want to believe terrible things will never happen to us. It will always be someone else's child who dies or someone else's house that burns to the ground. I have lived long enough and experienced enough in life to know that anything can happen to me or my family.

When my son Michael was ill with cancer, I really never believed he would die until it actually happened. But even though I didn't allow myself to believe he might die, I did sometimes try to imagine what it would be like to lose him.

I have done likewise with Glenna. I do not want Glenna to be deprived of going home to Jesus even at her young age, but I can't imagine myself raising our two young children without her. I find it difficult to believe that any other woman could love Sean and Megan as Glenna does. I think it is unlikely that any other woman would take the time off work and make all the trips to various doctors with Sean that Glenna does. I will sometimes question God, not really expecting an answer but trying to figure out why He does what He does even though I now it is impossible.

I can't begin to understand why God would give Glenna and me two precious children so late in our lives and then not let each of us live long enough to raise them into adulthood. I am reminded that God's ways are far above my ways. I am also reminded that God loves Megan and Sean even more than Glenna and I are capable of loving them, and the truth of the matter is God can take care of Sean and Megan perfectly without either Glenna or me. I pray daily that God will keep Glenna well, but I also pray that His will and not my will be done.

At the age of fifty-two years, I would guess that I have lived slightly more than half my life, assuming I eventually die of old age. I have seen enough of God's grace and mercy in my first fifty-two years to believe that no matter how long I live, His grace and mercy will be sufficient to see me through any trial that may come my way, including the possible premature death of my wife.

Book 2

It is now 2021. It has been nineteen years since *Years of Grace, Life of Mercy* was first published. I was fifty-two years of age at that writing, and I am now seventy-one years of age. I won't write about all that happened in the past nineteen years—it wasn't all that exciting— but I will share what I believe to be important situations and events where God has been with me. Many changes have taken place, and you may be surprised, maybe even amazed by some of the changes that have taken place.

First of all, I'd like to address the issue of anger. Over the years, I had occasions to become angry, some justified and some not so much. I can honestly say that I didn't always handle anger well, but I have not been controlled by anger. I continue to do my best to live as a Christian, and the Holy Spirit has been faithful to guide me. I don't get angry often, and it is short-lived. I have learned to never carry a grudge.

As I proceed to write, I'll be talking more about depression. Although some of what I write may sound like fiction, and I may not remember exactly how the events happened, I tell the truth, and the events did actually happen. I believe it will be entertaining and intriguing, but the object here is to show how God has and continues to be active in my life.

Before I begin writing about current events, I'd like to give you an update on Jim McTwiggin. In some month of 2013, I saw Jim's name and information on Facebook. I wrote him the following note:

Hi Jim, I can hardly believe how quickly time seems to pass. Some days seem really slow and I wonder if they will ever end. And yet, it has now been 50 years since we first met at Woodrow Wilson Junior High School in Council Bluffs. I'll admit, Jim, that I was never afraid of you, but it wasn't that you could have made mince meat out of me. It was because I believed that you never would. You were just too nice a person and I've always had a certain respect for you. If you haven't read my book, I think you would enjoy doing so. I hope to hear from you. Take care.

I later received this response from Jim:

Lar, I always liked you and your sister Linda, looks like yer doing great. I asked God to forgive me, you didn't deserve to be hurt. Yer a good man and I hope you can forgive me. I heard about your book, but I don't read much. I helped raise two great kids and married for 30 years, been on my own 14 years. Life isn't intended for man to be alone, but I do the best I can with my dog Daisy. I get bored and think about my childhood memories. Looks like we both have kids and kids that love us, and that is a wonderful gift.

It has been difficult for me to decide where to begin this next chapter (book 2). I decided to take a look at the journal that I have been keeping for many years. At that time, I had my own business and had been taking care of all the cosmetic work on cars at the Fox Chevrolet car dealership. This was my journal entry for May 14, 2008:

Yesterday I lost my account with Fox Dealership. Right now I am depressed and not thinking clearly. I am disappointed at my lack of faith. I believe God will get me through this, but I really hate feeling this way.

On May 17, 2008, I wrote,

> I'm still fighting depression and I'm uncertain what I'm going to do. It's almost impossible for me to go knocking on doors, looking for work, when I feel so depressed. I feel like someone punched me in the stomach and I can't seem to get rid of that feeling. I'm truly thankful for all who are praying for me. I'll go to church tomorrow and then pray that I'll find some work on Monday.

After a few weeks, I talked with the CEO at the Fox dealership. He told me that the dealership could no longer pay me as a Contractor, but he wanted me to go to work for the dealership as an employee. I was having very little success finding new accounts, so I let my business, Paint Team, LLC, go and went to work as a Fox employee. I was earning much-less money, but it was still a decent living.

On May 20, 2008, I made this journal entry:

> It rained today. I didn't leave the house except to go to Target with Glenna. After dinner I did force myself to go out and play ball with Sean for a short time. I spent most of the day lying around. Sometimes I'm on the verge of tears and feel sick to my stomach. I'm glad to see night come, but I dread the morning. I know I'm letting Glenna and our kids down. Glenna is strong though and she tries to encourage me. She is taking care of Sean and Megan because I'm just not there for them now. I read some of the Psalms and prayed for mercy. I do believe God is in this, but He does seem distant now. Where is

my faith, my strength? God, give me the gift of faith, undeserving as I am. I love you Lord.

As I looked back through my journal, I saw very few entries where I had mentioned anything about depression. The truth, though, is that I dealt on and off with depression for many years. I spent much time being counseled by psychiatrists and psychologists. Judging from my journal entries, Glenna and I were having some serious marital problems. I don't recall that my depression was the cause of any of our problems, but I'm sure it must have been. Glenna and I seldom fought or argued. I believed that each of us was happy in our marriage. I'm not sure when the friction between Glenna and I began.

On November 1, 2011, I made this entry in my journal:

> Glenna has been very cold towards me for some time now. This morning when I went to kiss her goodbye, she turned away from me. I asked her if she didn't like me. She said she loves me but doesn't like me. It was a painful thing to hear and leaves me wondering what to do.

Journal entry on December 10, 2011:

> On the evening of December 2nd Glenna and I had an argument. Sometime during our argument Glenna said to me that I was doing absolutely nothing to show Megan any love and affection. I love Megan dearly, so hearing these words from Glenna was extremely for me. It is hurtful for me to know that Megan would even think that I don't love her.

Sometime Friday evening, I overdosed on some antidepressants. I drove to the Fox dealership and drove my truck into a small paint booth in the body shop. The shop was closed, but I had a key to get in. I let my truck run for the entire night. I fell asleep in the truck bed. Morning had arrived, and I was still alive but very confused.

I walked over to the car lot and clocked in to go to work. I had no idea that it was Saturday morning. I must have looked pretty bad because the receptionist asked me if I was all right and asked me to sit down. Other people began to come in, and pretty soon, there was a crowd around me. They kept saying that they wanted to call 911, and I kept saying no, but someone called anyway, and I was soon being checked out by paramedics.

Our Lord had protected me and kept me alive for whatever reason. At that time, I had been in counseling with a psychiatrist, and I continued in counseling much longer. Every day, I was taking antidepressants. The antidepressants didn't appear to be helping me much. On one occasion, when I was seeing a new therapist, I told him that I would rather have cancer than be depressed. He told me that I was the second person to tell him that same thing. I continued to see a therapist for many more years and continued to take antide-pressants every day.

At a later date, I made another suicide attempt. I arrived home from my job on a late afternoon. For whatever reason, I was feeling really depressed. No one else was home. I pulled my work truck into the garage and closed the garage door. I left my truck running. I was pretty sure that I would no longer be alive after a few hours. I sat in my truck and just waited.

Soon it began to get very warm, and it was getting a little difficult for me to breathe. At some point, I got out of my truck, and I was lying face down on the cement floor. It was now very hot, and my clothes were soaking wet. I was having more difficult breathing, and I was thinking that I had to get some air.

The small garage door was about five yards from me. I knew that I had to get to it. I tried to push myself up from the floor, but all my strength was gone. I thought that if I could roll over, I could maybe make it to the door, but I didn't even have enough strength to roll over. I had given up.

I finally just laid my face down on the cement floor. It felt cold. I was sure that my life was over. I don't know how much time had passed, but I woke up, and I was lying next to the small garage door, which was now partly open. It was a hot summer day, but the air coming in through the partly open door felt very cool on my face and in my lungs. I was able to slowly get up onto my knees and crawl out the door. It seemed to be a short time before I felt recovered.

Every piece of my clothing was drenched. No one had come home yet. I went into the house through the back entrance and went up to my bedroom. I changed into dry clothes and went back downstairs. My wife and children soon arrived back home. I said nothing about what I had done. As far as I could tell, they had no idea that anything unusual had happened. I have no idea how I made it over to the garage door, and after I was there, I wouldn't have had enough strength to get up and open the door. Once again, our Lord had spared my life. Why? I do not know. Maybe, someday I will.

That was not my last attempt. On the morning of March 12, 2014, I walked out to my truck to go to work. Glenna and I crossed paths, and she ignored me. I stopped and looked at her and then asked her if she wanted a divorce. She told me that she didn't know. I took that as a yes! I drove to the Fox dealership, but I was extremely depressed. I still loved Glenna, and I did not want a divorce. My thinking wasn't clear, and I'm sure it was the depression talking, but I decided that there was no reason to continue living. I went to see the manager of the dealership and told him that I quit, and I did so right then.

I got into my truck and began to drive. I didn't care where I drove, but I ended up in Harrisburg, Pennsylvania. On the way there, I stopped at a liquor store and bought a six-pack of beer. It was a cold winter day, and there was a lot of ice on the ground. I pulled into the back of a large parking lot. There were no other cars nearby. I had an appointment with a psychologist that afternoon, and I had with me a bag of all the antidepressants I had been taking. I was going to talk with him to see if maybe I could stop taking at least a couple of them. I also had a single-edged razor blade with me because I used them in my work.

I locked my car doors and then swallowed many of the antidepressants. I then drank one can of beer and then took a razor blade and cut my wrist, not once but twice. I then remembered what a therapist had once told me. She told me that when a person commits suicide, it's people left behind who have to struggle the rest of their lives, thinking that maybe they were the cause, or maybe they could have done something to stop it from happening.

I then thought of Glenna, Megan, and Sean and decided that I could not go through with it. I was feeling very groggy, but I decided that I would just sleep for a while and then drive back home. I had done much more damage than I had realized, and it didn't work out that way.

I had no memory of what had happened. I had somehow gotten out of my truck and started to walk. I hadn't gotten far when I apparently slipped and hit my head on a concrete curb. In addition to the blood I had already lost, I was now bleeding from my head. I have no idea how long it had been since someone saw me and called for an ambulance.

The first thing I remembered is that I was lying on a gurney. It seemed like there were some other people around, and it seemed that we were still outside. I opened my eyes once and saw a lady looking down at me. I said, "You look like my sister."

I blacked out again, and when my eyes opened a second time, I saw her and said, "You are my sister." Some time must have passed because she had driven to Harrisburg, Pennsylvania, from Waldorf, Maryland, to get to me.

At some point, I heard someone—I thought it was a paramedic—say, "I don't know if this guy is going to make it."

Later, my sister told me that we were inside the hospital when I heard the man speak. There was no doubt that I was in a very serious condition. There was a specialist doctor there who wanted to give me an antidote to the antidepressants I had swallowed, but no one knew what I had taken, so there was nothing he could do. The hospital kept me in the intensive care unit.

Every day for the first three days, the doctor told my wife that I most likely wouldn't make it through the day. Glenna was sharing this information with my daughter, Megan. I did, however, and on the fourth day, I began to show some signs of improvement. When I finally woke up, I was in a regular hospital room. Once again, God had kept me alive.

A doctor in the hospital took me to a room where he was sitting and looking at information on a computer screen. He was apparently looking at my medical chart/history. He asked me if I knew why I was there in the hospital. I began to give him an answer, but he interrupted me and said, "I'll tell you why you are here. You were being overdosed on Effexor."

Sometime later, a different doctor told me the same thing. It was because I was being overdosed on Effexor (an antidepressant) that I had suicidal thoughts.

Glenna had been sharing the daily information she was receiving from the doctor that I probably wouldn't survive through the day. Of course, this was very disturbing news for Megan to have to hear. She thought she was going to lose her daddy. Sean, with Down syndrome, wasn't aware of what was happening. My two sons living in Omaha told me that they had their bags packed and were ready to fly to Maryland for my funeral.

I'm not sure how long I had been hospitalized, but I knew it had been a very long time, at least a month. During that time I was never visited or talked to by Glenna or Megan. But when I arrived back at my house, Glenna and Megan were not happy to see me. They were hurt and distraught when they thought that I was going to die, but now, they were very angry with me and even seemed to hate.

Subdural Hematoma

A few weeks after I had been released from the hospital, I began to feel some numbness in my right arm. I went to see a doctor and learned that I had a blood clot near my brain—subdural hematoma. It was probably a result of my falling and hitting my head on the concrete.I was told that subdural hematoma was very serious, and some people die as a result of having it. He told me that I needed to have surgery in order to have the blood clot removed. I put it off for a few weeks, but the numbness in my arm was getting worse, so I agreed to have the surgery. A small hole was drilled in my skull so the doctor could get to the blood clot and remove it. Even though the surgery was not actually on my brain, there were some negative effects I had to deal with.

When I awoke from surgery and was back in my regular hospital room, I quickly discovered that I had some paralysis in my right arm. I was given some food to eat. I picked up my fork, but whenI went to cut some meat, the fork was no longer in my hand. I hadn't realized that I had dropped it. I had to have a nurse help me eat.

What was really upsetting for me was that I couldn't talk. I didn't realize it at the time. To me, my speech sounded normal, but the people around me had no idea what I was saying. I was very upset, to say the least, because the doctor had given me no warning that these things might happen. I presumed that I was going to have to live this way for the rest of my life. I couldn't even write, not even one letter of the alphabet.

A doctor finally talked with me and assured me that the conditions were probably just temporary and that I would probably regain my ability to talk and have full use of my right arm. I spent time in physical therapy and even more time in speech therapy. I did eventually regain my ability to talk and was able to use my right arm.

I went back to the Fox car dealership and pleaded with them to give my job back to me. They did so, and I began doing more paintwork, but although I had regained the use of my right arm, it was still a little shaky. A steady hand is required to spray-paint a car, so it was difficult for me to do a good job. Therefore, I decided that it would be better for me to just retire, and I did so.

I stayed in the house, but I had retired from my job and was not working. I was continuing to see a therapist and continued to take antidepressants but no Effexor. Most of the time, I was lethargic. I mostly lay on the couch and didn't do much. Glenna and Megan ignored me as much as possible. Glenna didn't speak to me unless she absolutely had to. If I happened to pass Megan in a hallway, she would turn and face the wall so she wouldn't have to look at me. We continued to live this way for about a year. Life was not pleasant.

Arrest

On April 14, 2014, I was at my home in Damascus, Maryland. I received a telephone call from the central police station in Rockville, Maryland. I was told by the police officer calling that there was an issue in which my name had come up. I was asked to drive to the police station to get the matter cleared up.

I drove to the police station, and as soon as I walked into the station, I was arrested! Two officers handcuffed me and proceeded to escort me down the hallway. While we were walking, they asked me if I knew a Megan Caffery. I said yes, that she was my daughter. They told me that I was accused of sexually molesting my daughter. I could hardly believe what I was hearing.

They took me to an interrogation room and I was read my rights. I had done nothing wrong, so I told them I would answer their questions. I was badgered endlessly. I was interrogated separately by each officer. They did everything they could think of to get me to confess I sexually abused my daughter. Then I was told eleven charges had been filed against me, two of which were felonies. Each of the officers told me they had interrogated many people, knew that I was lying and that I was guilty of being a pedophile.

I asked the female officer if she had ever been wrong, and she indicated she had not. I demanded that I be given a polygraph test. They made arrangements for the polygraph test, and I was given the test right then. I was certain the matter would soon be settled.

After the test was completed, I was told the results were inconclusive. One of the officers told me that it didn't matter because I was going to jail anyway. Then I was put into a police car and driven to jail. I was put into a small cell and left there, not knowing what to expect next.

A few hours later, I was moved to an even smaller cell. I was made to strip completely, including my underwear. I was not allowed to keep anything, not even my watch. There was a two-inch piece of foam rubber on the concrete floor. That was to serve as my bed. There was another piece of foam rubber, which was to serve as my covering as I tried to sleep. There was no way to see outside this cell. A small slot was in the door, which was used to push in a tray of food. It was very humiliating, but fortunately, that was for just one night. I was moved to a somewhat-larger cell, where I was locked up for several days.

One day, I had to report to an officer of the court. It was her job to recommend to the judge what she thought the amount of my bail should be. She looked over the charges that had been made against me. First, she asked me when I was last arrested. I told her never! She then asked my age. She said, "You're sixty-six, and you have never been arrested?" She didn't believe me and had to look up my criminal record.

After seeing that I had never been arrested, she still had trouble believing the truth. She again looked at the charges that were made against me. She then said, "Because of the longevity of your crime, I'm going to recommend to the judge that your bail amount be no less than..."

I don't recall the exact dollar amount she stated, but she wanted to be sure that the high amount would keep me from being released. It seemed to me that everyone in the legal system assumed I was guilty, and I was treated as a pedophile.

Note: I would like to point out now that our Lord was with me through the entire time of my incarceration and court hearings. At least five miracles took place within the coming weeks. The next day after having stood before the court official who recommended my high bail amount, I was standing in front of the judge. A court-appointed lawyer was standing next to me.

Miracle 1: The lawyer said something to the judge, but I wasn't listening. I was just waiting to hear the bad news. The judge then told me that if I were to be found guilty of every charge, I could be sentenced to up to thirty years in prison. The judge then used a legal term that I was not familiar with, probably some Latin term. I had to ask the lawyer next to me what the judge's judgment was. She told me that I was going to be released until my trial date without paying anything. I was then released from jail and was told I had to report to a probation officer two times a week.

On my second visit with him, he asked me how I was doing. I told him that I was doing okay but that I'd be doing better if I didn't have to drive to see him two times a week. Miracle 2. He told me it would be okay if I saw him only once a week. This is unheard of for an assumed pedophile.

I hired an attorney, and he began working to prepare for my trial. Over the next couple of months, I had to appear in court several times. Nothing significant was ever done, except a new court date being set. Information had been exchanged between my attorney and the Maryland state attorney who was representing my accusers. The state attorney was looking under every rock, trying to find evidence to use against me. She even had my personal computer confiscated from my house. I know that she found nothing there because the charges made against me were false.

My attorney and I were finally given a date on which my trial was to begin. I could not even imagine how things would unfold in the courtroom. On that date, my attorney and I were standing before the judge. I didn't realize it at the time, but my accusers weren't even in the courtroom. The judge reminded me that if I had been guilty of every one of the charges made against me, I could be sentenced for up to thirty years in prison. My first thought was that I would certainly die in prison. The judge then said, "All the charges have been dropped."

Miracle 3: Both my attorney and I were shocked—he more so than I. When we were back in my attorney's office, he told me that felony charges were never, ever just dropped. He told me that he had been practicing law for over twenty-six years and had never seen or heard of a felony charge just being dropped.

Miracle 4: My attorney then told me that he was amazed that the court hadn't required me to wear an ankle bracelet. He told me that the court wants to know the exact location of a suspected pedophile every second of every day.

Miracle 5: It takes at least five years before a request can be made to have a criminal record expunged. Within the first year, all charges made against me were expunged. I was told that there was no record that I had been arrested.

Reason False Charges
Were Made

This is very difficult to share because it was my wife and seventeen-year-old daughter who made the false charges. I do not want to do anything to harm them, but I do have to tell the truth about all that happened in order to share how our Lord was with me through the entire ordeal, even to the point of attempted suicide.

I believe that there were even more attempts that I have not shared. I'm sure Glenna remembers each that she was aware of. After one attempt, I promised Glenna that I would never make another attempt. However, about a year later, I did make another attempt. It was my last attempt that I shared, where I overdosed on Effexor. Glenna chose not to believe that I had been overdosed on Effexor.

I am acutely aware that I caused my wife, daughter, and many others much sorrow and pain. I'm sure Glenna thought it was going to happen again, and to prevent herself and my daughter from being hurt again, she tried to get me out of her life. I understand what they did to me is just unthinkable, downright evil. I knew I could never trust Glenna again. She even managed to turn my son Sean against me.

On September 2017, with the approval of the pastors of the Christian church that I was attending, I filed for divorce. I believed that I had little reason to remain in Maryland, so in about mid-April in 2018, I packed up my belongings and moved to Omaha, Nebraska, where my sons Steve and Tim, from my first marriage, live.

This may even be miracle 6. For the past three years that I have been living in Omaha, I have had no need for any counseling or need for any antidepressants. If anyone reading my story happens to know my wife Glenna and my daughter Megan, please hold nothing against them. I don't, and I hold no grudge against them. I believe that what they need is to feel the love and peace of Jesus. I have had no communication with Glenna, Sean, or Megan for the past three years, but I love and pray for each of them daily.

It is obvious to me that God has kept me alive in spite of myself. He does have a purpose for me, as He does for each of us, but I have yet determined what it is. Maybe He just wants me to share with people all that He has done and continues to do in my life. I do want to encourage people.

As for depression, I really don't understand it. I have been told that it is a disease, that it is a chemical imbalance in the brain, etc. It can be affected by the way we think. It has caused many problems for me, but at this time, I am not depressed, so please be encouraged by that. Depression does not last forever. If you feel depressed, do not be embarrassed or ashamed. Get help, especially if you are feeling suicidal. Suicide is never the answer. Listen to your doctor, and above all else, listen to God and pray.

I'm sure you'd like to know how the story ends, but only God knows the ending. I do believe it will be happy. I am happy now. I am still a diamond in the rough, and God has much more work to do in my life. I continue to thank Him for the years of grace and life of mercy.

Grace is defined by the dictionary as merited assistance given for his regeneration or sanctification. Sanctification is the daily process of becoming more like Jesus.

Mercy is defined by the dictionary as a blessing that is an act of divine favor or compassion. Mercy implies compassion that forbears punishing, even when justice demands it—clemency. I believe that because of God's mercy, every one of my countless sins is forgiven. I will never receive the punishment I truly deserve, but when my life on this earth is over, I will spend eternity with Jesus, not because of what I did but because of what He did.

About the Author

Larry E. Caffery currently lives alone in Omaha, Nebraska, but is in a serious relationship with a very lovely lady, Nana, who helped with the completion of his book. He has four adult children. Larry is hopeful that the readers of his book will be encouraged to have a closer relationship with our Lord.

www.ingramcontent.com/pod-product-compliance
Lightning Source LLC
Chambersburg PA
CBHW021002150626
46549CB00012BA/939